Praise for
When You Love Too Much

Steve's insightful writings on delicate and demanding themes have helped so many. If this book's title addresses a personal issue you've wrestled with, it's likely you will find counsel and practical wisdom in *When You Love Too Much*.

Jack W. Hayford
Author, *Fatal Attractions* and *The Anatomy of Seduction*
Founding Pastor, The Church On The Way
Van Nuys, California

If readers do not fully comprehend the meaning of sexual, romantic and love addiction after reading this simply written book, they never will. Nothing better has crossed my desk on this subject. We need it now.

Dr. Yvonne Kaye
Author, *Credit, Cash and Co-Dependency* and *The Child That Never Was*
Speaker

In addition to providing a helpful and insightful overview of the problems of sex and love addiction, *When You Love Too Much* outlines steps toward recovery. There is hope.

Dale Ryan
CEO, Christian Recovery International

when you love too much

Stephen Arterburn

Regal

From Gospel Light
Ventura, California, U.S.A.

PUBLISHED BY REGAL BOOKS
FROM GOSPEL LIGHT
VENTURA, CALIFORNIA, U.S.A.
PRINTED IN THE U.S.A.

Regal

Regal Books is a ministry of Gospel Light, a Christian publisher dedicated to serving the local church. We believe God's vision for Gospel Light is to provide church leaders with biblical, user-friendly materials that will help them evangelize, disciple and minister to children, youth and families.

It is our prayer that this Regal book will help you discover biblical truth for your own life and help you meet the needs of others. May God richly bless you.

For a free catalog of resources from Regal Books/Gospel Light, please call your Christian supplier or contact us at 1-800-4-GOSPEL *or* www.regalbooks.com.

Originally published as *Addicted to Love* by Servant Publications in 1991.

All Scripture quotations, unless otherwise indicated, are taken from the *Holy Bible, New International Version®*. Copyright © 1973, 1978, 1984 by International Bible Society. Used by permission of Zondervan Publishing House. All rights reserved.

The names and characterizations in this book are fictional, although based on real events. Any similarity between the names and characterizations with real people is unintended and purely coincidental.

Any omission of credits is unintentional. The publisher requests documentation for future printings.

Servant Publications edition published in 1991.
Regal edition published in December 2004.

Cover design by David Griffing

Library of Congress Cataloging-in-Publication Data
Arterburn, Stephen, 1953–
  [Addicted to "love"]
  When you love too much / Stephen Arterburn.—Regal ed.
    p. cm.
  Originally published: Addicted to "love". Ann Arbor, Mich. : Servant Publications, c1991.
  ISBN 0-8307-3514-3 (hardcover), 0-8307-3623-9 (trade paperback)
  1. Relationship addiction—Religious aspects—Christianity. 2. Sex addiction—Religious aspects—Christianity. I. Title.

  BV4596.R43A78 2004b
  248.8′6—dc22   2004023534

1   2   3   4   5   6   7   8   9   10   /   10   09   08   07   06   05   04

Rights for publishing this book in other languages are contracted by Gospel Light Worldwide, the international nonprofit ministry of Gospel Light. Gospel Light Worldwide also provides publishing and technical assistance to international publishers dedicated to producing Sunday School and Vacation Bible School curricula and books in the languages of the world. For additional information, visit www.gospellightworldwide.org; write to Gospel Light Worldwide, P.O. Box 3875, Ventura, CA 93006; or send an e-mail to info@gospellightworldwide.org.

Dedication

To the thousands of people who believed that what they were pursuing was love, but found it was not, I dedicate this book.

I pray that you will find in these pages the hope and motivation to change. May you also find true, unconditional love and acceptance and share it with another fellow struggler.

Contents

Acknowledgments

I appreciate the intense efforts of Katie Temple in researching, editing and developing material. She has been an irreplaceable help in this project.

Lisa Adair, my assistant, has been a faithful example of self-sacrifice, personal integrity and dedication to God's best.

John Blattner took the final draft and edited it into a readable book. His skills have greatly enhanced the message.

Ann Spangler and Beth Feia have my utmost appreciation for searching me out, suggesting the book and sticking by me through this long process of writing.

I am greatly indebted to all those who shared their lives openly and honestly to help me understand this problem.

Introduction

Have we overdone it? Have we carried the addiction craze too far?

No one questions that alcohol and drug use can become addictive. But what about romance? Destructive relationships? Even sex? Do these belong in the same category as a shot of bourbon or a line of cocaine? And if so, does recovery from these "people addictions" work the same way as it does for an alcoholic or drug addict? Are we coming to understand these problems in a new light? Or are we just putting a new label on an old predicament?

These are questions that scholars, researchers, theologians and therapists—not to mention those struggling with compulsive behavior around sex, romance and relationships—have been grappling with in recent years. There has been much talk of sex as an addiction, an addiction to romance or an addiction to destructive relationships that drives people to give up what is healthy in themselves in order to feed what is unhealthy in others. Our headlines have been filled with news of well-known individuals—from preachers to politicians—whose careers are veering out of control because of shocking and inexplicable actions and behaviors.

What is really going on? Why do these things happen? Getting at the truth isn't always easy. Unwitting, preconceived notions can distort otherwise objective examinations of reality—especially in such areas as sex, where everyone considers themselves an expert. Looking in the wrong places can also lead us to wrong answers. Yesterday's textbooks lack insight into today's sex-saturated society and into the behaviors that uniquely characterize a post-sexual-revolution generation.

The answers I offer in this book do not come from modern-day pseudo-authorities or outdated texts. I began my study with men and women haunted by behaviors that they once controlled but that eventually came to control them. These individuals were brave enough to confront what they had become and to draw conclusions about what this meant for their futures.

I have met these men and women in self-help groups, in treatment centers, in churches, universities and seminaries. They have shared with me their despair and their hope, and have allowed me to present their struggles in the ensuing pages. I am most grateful for their openness, courage and hope. From their pain, I hope to derive new understandings of old problems and new solutions to old predicaments. To protect their anonymity, their names and some of the circumstances of their lives have been changed.

The stories I will tell you often contain details that may make some readers uncomfortable. My intent is not to shock readers but to examine carefully and candidly how addictions progress, and to describe the dark and troubled world in which addicts live. If you suspect that someone you love may be in danger of addiction, these stories may open your eyes to some hard realities and offer insights into how to approach the problem. If you suspect that you, yourself, are suffering from unhealthy dependencies, these stories may help you make an honest assessment of your need and encourage you on the road of recovery. Recovery is never intended to be a *self-help* proposition. It is meant to be a matter of getting out of the way and letting God help us at long last.

A Personal Confession

I am able to draw on one other source of insight into the problems of love and sex addiction. That source is my own experience—one that I deeply regret. Yet I am thankful that it has forced me to grow up and to learn how tough the reality of life can be.

My story begins in the 1970s. I was unmarried and lonely, working in a psychiatric hospital while going to seminary to study to be a counselor. I had no close relationships and was accountable to no one. I had just been abandoned by a very important woman in my life. My discouragement and depression were deep.

Some would have responded to my situation by going out and getting drunk or by drugging up to mask the pain. Others might have resorted to an eating binge. For me, solace came from a woman—a married woman.

She took an interest in me. In my pain, I responded eagerly. Her presence, her voice, her touch were like a salve for my broken heart. I never planned to have an intimate relationship with her, let alone a sexual one. I just wanted to be near her, to be reminded of what it felt like to matter to someone. Not realizing how weak and vulnerable I was, I sought out her attention. She gave it to me, which made me feel whole.

As I look back from the vantage point of several years, I can easily see how this relationship progressed to a sexual affair. But at the time, in the midst of my pain, I was blind to what lay ahead.

When I was not with her, I thought about her day and night. I was obsessed with her. I couldn't concentrate on anything. I would do whatever I had to do to get away from work and talk to her, in person or on the phone. I craved her presence the way a drug addict craves heroin. When we were together, I felt energized, as though I could conquer the world. When our times together ended, I slumped into withdrawal and depression.

It was really self-obsession—an obsession with my own pain—that led to obsession with this woman. Had I not been so consumed with the hurt and mistreatment I felt I had suffered, I would not have grasped so desperately at the quick fix of a hopelessly wrong relationship.

In fact, it was the very intensity of my pain that made so dangerous a relationship seem necessary. The intoxication of romance seemed stronger in a forbidden romance with a married woman. A more conventional relationship, it seemed, would not have provided the necessary relief.

The spiraling need for greater risk and more intense romantic intoxication inevitably led to sexual involvement. Every time we were together, I soared out of my depression and fear into a rapture that seemed like utter security. But those ecstasies quickly wore off, and I plunged once more into an abyss of guilt and shame even more painful than the inner hurt that had launched the process in the first place. In the attempt to salve my wound, I only made it worse.

My attempts to treat my pain only fueled my obsession. I plunged into a vicious cycle, coming back to the relationship for relief from the very pain that the relationship itself caused. I somehow persuaded myself—in the face of everything I had learned about right and wrong, and in the face of my own Christian convictions—that it was okay to be with another man's wife. Their marriage, I rationalized, was in trouble anyway. Besides, I *needed* her. I was as hooked on the relationship as any alcoholic is hooked on booze.

To this day, I cannot say what ultimately led us to see how hopeless and wrong our relationship had become, and to bring it to an end. It was the grace of God to be sure. I also cannot say what led us to accept and act on that grace after so resolutely turning our backs on it for so long. However, we did act, and we both finally found the courage to put a stop to our relationship and get on with our lives.

Facing the pain of separation was not easy. Our lives were never the same afterward. I know I am forgiven for what I did—that this sin, like all my sin, is somehow covered in the incredible mercy of God. I know this. But there are still times when I do not *feel* God's forgiveness. There are days when I flash back to those selfish, pain-filled times, when the crushing weight of depression and self-pity comes over me again. The feelings of remorse seem to diminish by degrees, but they never disappear entirely.

I pray for this woman and for the others that were damaged by my selfish mistake. I have taken great care that it never happens again. By God's grace, it has not. What could easily have become an initial instance of a destructive and repetitious pattern stopped after one occurrence.

I learned many things from this tragic episode. I learned how vulnerable I am—how vulnerable we all are—even in a context of firm moral convictions and noble intentions. I learned that in times of stress or disappointment, I must consciously involve myself in healthy pursuits and relationships that will help me deal constructively with my problems, rather than let myself slide into unhealthy ones.

I learned how sickening our secrets can be and how they distort our perception of reality and our ability to deal with it. For years after the relationship ended, I was miserable from keeping it hidden. Once I was able to confess what I had done, I experienced tremendous relief.

I also learned how powerful addiction can be. I used to think that only drugs and alcohol could take people captive. Now I know that other things can be just as enslaving.

Most important, I learned that no matter how grievous our sin, God is faithful to forgive us and deliver us when we turn to Him. Through Him, I have been able to recover from the mess I created.

I became dependent on romance, on a wrong relationship and on sex to help me cope with the pain of human existence. In seeking relief, I brought upon myself more despair than I have ever known, before or since. I wish no one would ever have to experience the desolation I knew. It is with that wish in mind that I write this book. I hope it can serve as an instrument of God's grace for those who are already trapped in one of the "people addictions," or who are flirting with the temptations that those addictions bring.

CHAPTER 1

marisa's story

Ugly, dumb and fat.

Marisa's brother hung those labels on her when she was just six years old. By the time Marisa was 12, she was living up to (or down to) each of them. She was almost 30 pounds overweight and struggling to maintain a C average in school. Marisa felt out of place everywhere she went. It was impossible to make friends. No one, it seemed, made any effort to relate to her. She drew back from others in the gloomy certainty that no one would be interested in her anyway.

Marisa suffered in silence, longing for someone to provide her with the love and affection she craved. But no such person appeared. More and more, she turned to food in search of comfort. As Marisa's brother continued to torment her with his cruel indictments, she fell farther behind in school and grew more obese year by year.

Marisa's brother had not developed his critical nature on his own but had simply learned from the example of their father—a merchant marine who was often away for three to six months at a stretch.

Whenever he was at home, he ranted, condemned, judged and put others down constantly, until his next journey took him away. The moment he left, Marisa's brother took over the role of emotional tormenter. She had no respite.

While she was in the sixth grade, Marisa later recalled, she began taking refuge in a fantasy world all her own. It seemed harmless enough at first. But before long it became her "drug of choice." The more her brother and father made reality miserable, the more solace she found in her make-believe world. Her fantasies became a kind of salve, a way to soothe the pain of living in a family that could not, or would not, give her the acceptance and affirmation she needed.

It began one day when Marisa was rummaging around in the attic and came across a book she had seen her mother reading. She picked it up and thumbed through the pages, then sat down and began to read the first chapter. She was immediately fascinated by the story, about two people who met on an island in the Caribbean and fell head over heels in love. The instant they set eyes on each other, it seemed, they completely forgot about the families and responsibilities they had left behind in the real world, and tumbled headlong into each other's lives. Each had been grievously hurt before. But in one another's arms, all the pain was magically erased.

Marisa's head was swimming. The book seemed to confirm something she had instinctively known all along but had never known how to put into words: Love and affection from the right kind of man would instantly and permanently wipe away all her pain and confusion.

From then on Marisa made frequent trips to the attic. Her mother had stored a huge pile of novels there, and she wanted to read them all. The plot was invariably the same—only the names of the characters and some details of the setting seemed to change. But this only made Marisa's excursions into her dream world that much more safe and reliable.

In her mind, Marisa became each of the heroines she read about, placing herself in their circumstances, sharing their hurts and participating in their euphoria as one handsome, exotic man after another swept them off their feet and lifted them above their pain.

She spent hours poring over her mother's book collection. In the process Marisa learned a great deal about seduction—how to seduce and how to be seduced. The language of illicit love became almost second nature to her private thoughts.

Marisa also came to realize that all the heroines in the books were unlike her in one crucial respect: They were all slim and trim. If she stayed at her current weight, no man would ever come for her as the men in the books did—to turn her fantasies into reality and deliver her from her nightmare existence. The more Marisa thought about it, the more convinced she became that only her obesity stood in the way of her deliverance. She had to lose weight.

At first Marisa tried dieting. She cut back on her eating, or at least tried to, and made a few feeble attempts at exercise. It didn't work. In fact, it seemed that the more she tried not to eat, the more desperate for food she became. Eating and reading romance novels had become her only forms of escape.

> When she was with a boy, Marisa would simply play a role drawn from her built-in encyclopedia of romantic fantasy.

But Marisa soon learned a new skill that was to prove remarkably effective: She learned how to make herself throw up after eating. It was the best of both worlds. Now she could eat as much as she wanted, whenever she wanted, and still have the kind of figure she knew she had to have.

By the time summer came around, Marisa had shed most of her excess pounds. For the first time in her life, she looked good and felt comfortable in a swimsuit. Everyone commented on how cute she looked—everyone except her brother, that is, who continued to harp on her clumsiness and stupidity. But Marisa was increasingly able to tune out his negative comments. Comfort and affirmation, she believed, would soon come her way from other sources.

She was not disappointed. As Marisa's body became more attractive, boys began to notice her. She got as much attention as the heroines in her mother's books. She loved it. When she was with a boy, Marisa would simply play a role drawn from her built-in encyclopedia of romantic fantasy.

The more boys flirted with her, the more she became convinced that they were the answer to her problems. She felt good about herself when—and, increasingly, only when—she was with a guy. The obvious next step was to secure a full-time boyfriend as soon as possible.

That was where Brad came in.

Brad lived three streets over from Marisa. He was not especially good-looking or popular, and he was a bully. He spent most of his time with his older brother, who was going into tenth grade, and looked down his nose at the activities of kids his own age. Brad acted as though the rest of the world existed to measure up to his standards. Nothing and no one was ever good enough for him.

What this elicited from Marisa was an overwhelming drive to meet Brad's demanding standards and find acceptance in his eyes. She felt almost compelled to be with him, to attach herself to him. She stalked him as a hunter stalks his prey. Though only 12 years old, Marisa's reading had taught her the techniques of a mature woman who was out to find a man.

When Marisa's thirteenth birthday came, Brad was allowed to take her to a movie alone. But they never made the long walk to the theater. Instead they spent the time in the back of his brother's car, parked in the driveway of Brad's house. It was tumbling and awkward, but by duplicating all she had read during those long hours in the attic, Marisa was able to complete her first sexual experience.

Later she would reflect on how appropriate it was that her first sexual encounter should be with an angry, abusive male—just like her father and brother. Marisa would come to realize she was trying to make up for the emotional intimacy she had never known with them by sharing physical intimacy with Brad.

Every significant male in her life had been cruel and abusive. Not surprisingly, her image of God was also negative and critical. Marisa assumed God did not love her and would surely punish her for the things she was doing. But the prospect of punishment didn't matter. Those moments of being close to someone, of being wanted, were her antidote to a lifetime of pain. She felt no guilt or remorse, only relief—and the desire to experience that relief as often as possible.

Marisa's whole destructive cycle was tied up with destructive men. It seemed a cruel irony that while hypercritical men were the root of her problem, she sought out precisely such men as the solution to her problem.

Because of her bulimic behavior patterns, Marisa managed to keep her weight at a fairly constant 110 pounds through her sixteenth year. Her dependency on men grew throughout this period. She looked to them for security, for release from the pain that gnawed at her. Virtually every new boy she met became the object of her desire. Her mood would change as the quest for male gratification took control of her thoughts and feelings. In those moments of sexual intimacy she felt free from her hurts and good about herself.

But it was also during her sixteenth year that Marisa's fragile life was further traumatized. Her reputation at school and around town could not have been worse. Everyone knew she was "easy." She saw the knowing looks and overheard the whispered comments.

She decided to prove to herself and to everyone else that they were wrong about her—that she couldn't be taken for granted, couldn't be simply used and then discarded by any boy that came along. On one particular night Marisa made up her mind: She would keep herself, and the situation, under control. She would neither encourage nor respond to any sexual overtures.

It was no use. The boy she was with knew her reputation and knew exactly what he wanted from her. When she refused to give it willingly, he took it forcefully. He raped her, then left her in the middle of a field as he drove away.

Marisa had to walk back to town alone. She was hurt and crying, but she was determined to act as if the event had not fazed her. She stuffed the rage she felt deep inside. No one else would ever know what had happened or how it had hurt. She felt proud of her ability to swallow the grief and pain, to let nothing show.

But she was unable to bury her feelings for very long. Finally the anger and depression she tried so hard to suppress rose up and overwhelmed her, and she tried to commit suicide by swallowing a bottle of her mother's sleeping pills. Her brother found her lying unconscious and took her to the emergency room to have her stomach pumped. Later he ridiculed her for not being smart enough to even kill herself without being found out.

As a result of her suicide attempt, Marisa was assigned to a counselor. But the counselor was inadequate to deal with the awful tangle of problems in Marisa's tortured soul. She soon returned to her pattern of seeking out a man to provide a quick fix for her problems. One man after another used and abused her, each taking a little of her self-worth when he left. But Marisa never stopped looking for her Prince Charming, the man who she believed could fix her and make her better once and for all.

By the time she was 24, Marisa had been through dozens of destructive relationships and hundreds of sexual encounters. She had become pregnant three times and had all three pregnancies aborted. She had also contracted herpes.

That diagnosis finally got her attention. When the doctor told Marisa she had herpes, she realized that if she continued on the same path, contracting AIDS was just as likely a consequence. Utterly broken, struggling just to get through each day, she decided there had to be a better way. Determined to find a way out of her nightmare, she made the difficult decision to change. When she finally reached the point when she wanted freedom so badly that she was willing to pay any price for it, recovery became a possibility for the first time.

People Addictions

Marisa's story illustrates all three of the addictions we will be discussing in this book. She started with romance—the fantasy life she constructed from her mother's lurid novels. Before long, she tried to find in real life the kind of intimacy and security she had read about. In a futile search for someone who would make up for the unmet needs of her childhood, she attached herself to one man after another and soon became hooked on sex and the escape it seemed to provide.

Passion is like energy. It can be used for good purposes or bad.

When Marisa came to a treatment center, she was in a state of severe depression and wanted no part of group involvement or interaction with the staff. She did, however, want to recover. Her desire for a better life ultimately lifted her out of her isolation and into a process of change and growth.

After a long struggle with her compulsive behavior patterns and her bulimia, Marisa is at last beginning to enjoy the life she wants. She attends one of more than 2,000 meetings held each week for those recovering from romance, relationship and sex addictions.

The number of people like Marisa grows each year, as does the number of groups catering to their needs. There is a growing hope for those who have become enslaved to romantic fantasy, destructive relationships and sexual involvement.

Victims of Passion

Those who suffer from people addictions are victims of their own passion. Now, passion of the soul is no more evil than is appetite. Passion is like energy. It can be used for good purposes or bad.

Passion motivates us to achieve greatness, to go beyond normal limits, to excel, to spend ourselves for others.

Passion motivates an order of nuns to feed the poor and comfort the dying.

Passion motivates the mother of a learning-disabled child to spend hours working on a single verbal skill.

Passion motivates a devoted husband to care for a wife suffering from Alzheimer's disease.

Yet passion has another side. Turned to wrong purposes, it can land someone in bed with hundreds of strangers and leave that person with incurable diseases and a trail of broken relationships.

The Root Addiction?

Romance, relationships and sex are only three of many all-consuming addictive preoccupations of our culture. Addictions to food, money, power, alcohol and drugs grip millions of people in our "you can have it all" society. And although the consequences of any compulsion or addiction can destroy a person, it seems that romance, relationship and sex addictions strike at the heart of human development and strip the individual of any sense of self-worth.

Indeed, some experts believe that these people addictions—romance, relationships, sex—are the root addictions and that all other addictions stem from them. In this view, people craving romantic attachment or sex turn to alcohol or drugs as a more acceptable way to cope with pain and emptiness.

As people addictions progress, the victimization of others also increases. The fuel for the compulsion is always another person. It may be a molested child, a betrayed spouse, an abandoned lover or a one-night stand who sought a relationship but found only deception and manipulation. Even in the case of pornography and the compulsive masturbation that follows it—a seemingly "solitary" and "victimless" activity—the user pays for the magazine, video or Internet service in order to compensate the exploited "performers."

The essential question is asked in the title of Tina Turner's hit song, "What's Love Got to Do with It?" Those recovering from romance, relationship and sex addictions come to realize that love—authentic, genuine, self-sacrificing love, as opposed to the tawdry substitutes that so often usurp the name—had nothing to do with their compulsive behavior. They had become enslaved in a futile search for security or relief from pain, or in playing out a "victimizer" role learned as a child victim.

Only when the compulsion is acknowledged, only when recovery is initiated, is there any hope for an authentic love relationship. Then there is hope for self-acceptance and for sharing who you truly are with another human being.

Recovery is a journey—a journey toward a mended heart, a healed soul and a mind no longer torn by the tyranny of passion. Those who travel that path of recovery regain the freedom to make healthy choices. It is a journey that many who were once addicted to love have successfully completed—a journey this book will help you make, too.

CHAPTER 2

Hooked on Romance

Roxanne hated sex.

She had read over and over that women wanted and needed sex just as much as men did, but she didn't believe it. The very thought of sexual intercourse repulsed her. She never pursued men with the desire to be sexual with them. That was the last thing she wanted.

And yet, Roxanne did pursue men, and she did have sex with them. That she would put herself through an experience she found so distasteful was a measure of her desperation, of her willingness to do whatever she had to do to fill the aching void in her soul. That void, she had decided, was caused by the emotional neglect of a father too aloof to be concerned with his daughter's needs for affection.

That neglect prompted Roxanne to "act out" sexually at an early age. She lost her virginity when she was 14 to a neighbor boy three years her senior. It was a hurried affair in a vacant house down the street. There was no affection, no feeling of love—just the process of completing the act as one would any other bodily function. Neither she nor the boy said anything afterwards; indeed, they never spoke to each other again.

Roxanne's uneventful, confusing flight from virginity had a negative impact on her sexuality for years to come. The older she got, the more distasteful sex became. It was the vulnerability of sex that was so hard to handle.

Roxanne tried to avoid sex entirely. She went from one relationship to another, flirtatiously revving up the sexual engines of her male companions, and then shutting them down if they wanted to go "too far." The men, of course, were confused and frustrated over her seductive behavior, which was immediately turned off when reciprocal advances were offered. Before long they got fed up with the ritual and left her. Roxanne would simply move on to someone else, constantly in need of male attention to fill her inner emptiness.

One night Roxanne met a wealthy man at a Beverly Hills party. He was married but not with his wife. They talked for an hour before he left with some business associates. During that hour she was intoxicated from his attention, drunk on the fantasies and dreams that flooded her mind. The thought of him became her newest source of relief and led her through the familiar process of romance addiction one more time.

The day after the party, Roxanne still could not get her mind off the man she had met. She thought about him every moment, about where he lived and where he worked. The ache in her heart seemed to grow as she imagined how happy she could be with him. Her job at a local department store suddenly seemed unimportant in comparison. She could barely concentrate on her customers. At day's end she had sold nothing.

That night as Roxanne sat at her table, she kept thinking of this man. She wondered what he was doing. She imagined him fighting with his wife, whom she pictured as a shrewish woman who made his life miserable. She pictured him promising his daughters that one day he would find them a better mother. She imagined their wedding and the blissful life they would have together. She had retreated into the world of "what might be." What actually was reality no longer mattered.

After a night of fitful sleep, Roxanne did not feel like going to work. She called in sick and then lay in bed until 10—when her obsession finally drove her to action.

She got up, showered and put on a conservative but attractive dress. Then she drove downtown to stage a "chance" meeting with the man of her dreams. Roxanne drove by his office building around 11, figuring out how she might casually run into him as he left for lunch. She parked her car and went inside, where she took a seat on a granite bench facing the building's elevators. Anyone going out to lunch would have to come out of one of those elevators and walk through the lobby.

She waited for more than an hour. When he finally appeared Roxanne went into action like an accomplished actress. She literally bumped into him as he passed and then, acting flustered and embarrassed, invited him to join her for lunch. He accepted. They took a cab to a nearby restaurant. The hunt had been a success. Roxanne had selected her target and patiently stalked him. For the two hours they were together she felt as though she were in heaven. The gnawing emptiness was gone.

As they rode back from the restaurant, Roxanne mentioned that she had two tickets to a play that weekend. Was there any way he could get free from his obligations and join her? Yes, he said, there was. She dropped off one ticket at his office. They met at the theater, in their seats, shortly after the house lights had been dimmed. At intermission he slipped away to the lobby before the lights came up and then returned to his seat when the theater was again darkened. The awkward ritual did not bother Roxanne. On the contrary, she found it exciting.

The play seemed to last forever. All she wanted was for it to be over so they could be together. Roxanne whispered her invitation to him to come to her apartment. When he nodded his acceptance, she felt like a third-grader who had just won a spelling bee. She had met the man of her dreams, pursued him and captured him. Soon he would be with her. Her fantasy was coming true.

Soft music and warm candlelight set the scene as Roxanne pursued her romantic ritual. They talked. They laughed. He had never done anything like this before, he said. Soon, however, his awkwardness faded and he grew more and more comfortable.

Then, just when he was sure he knew what was to come next, Roxanne announced that it was time for him to leave. He looked at her quizzically. He wasn't ready to go, but agreed anyway, promising to call her soon. Roxanne felt satisfied, completed. Her plan had worked; her dream had been fulfilled. She had drawn him into her life and won his affection. He had promised to call her again. She felt like a new woman.

Roxanne couldn't help but smile as she drew her bath. She thought of what she would do the next day. There would be no chase, no hunt; there wouldn't be a need for it. And there would be no recounting her evening's activities to friends or coworkers. She had no desire to share with anyone what had happened. The secrecy, in fact, was part of the appeal. Roxanne went to bed thinking of the man whose presence had brought her such comfort and relief.

She did not, however, feel that wonderful when she woke up the next morning. Roxanne felt frustrated and confused. Flashes of guilt raced through her as she envisioned the man with his wife and family. But she did not want to admit there had been anything wrong in what she had done. Surely there must be some problem in his marriage or he would not have responded to her. She reminded herself of the articles she had read about affairs actually helping marriages. That was it: far from being a potential source of trouble, she was helping this man.

Try as she might, however, she could not justify her actions. She needed someone to blame for her chronic inability to carry on a normal relationship with a normal, unmarried man. Her father was the easiest target. He had not met her needs. He had not provided her with the love to which she was entitled. It was all his fault.

This was a line of thought she had pursued many times before, the script of a play that she had long since committed to memory. She was as focused now on her father's neglect of her as she had been for the last 10 years. He had cheated her out of a normal childhood. He had driven her to seek what happiness she could in forbidden romances. Roxanne was ruthless with her blaming. She gave no thought to her own responsibility for the choices she made. Her problems were all the fault of her father. Because of the way he had undermined her life, she felt as if she were somehow owed something—and it was from the men who happened into her life that she demanded the payments on her emotional ransom.

Day after day Roxanne continued to pursue her latest quarry. Drinks after work, walks in the park, meetings in secret places—he came each time she called. When they were together she felt transported out of her misery, the object of a desirable man's affection and longing. But when they were apart, she found herself in more pain than ever. She thought of her mother's bitter prediction that she would come to no good.

At these moments Roxanne felt deep, penetrating shame. She indeed felt "good for nothing," deserving of all the guilt she could inflict upon her battered soul. As the intoxicating feelings of romance wore off, she would run head-on into the wall of reality and come face-to-face with her dark and devious side.

Roxanne wanted desperately to escape the tyranny of her shame. But she saw no way out. The spiral of emptiness, filled by hollow romantic rituals that in the end only produced greater emptiness, was by now second nature. She had known abandonment and loneliness in childhood and she could not bear the thought of experiencing it again.

She still remembered the long, tortured hours of wondering if her father cared for her, all the while knowing that he did not. Anything was better than that. Or was it? In the end her depression would drive her to thoughts of suicide—and then, inevitably, back to the familiar hunt for a romantic "fix."

Each time one of these cycles had played itself out, Roxanne promised herself that this was the last time. She would find a counselor. She would confide in a friend. She would join a group where she could talk about her problems, get some encouragement and listen to advice. Above all, she would stay away from men, especially married men. No more infatuations. No more seduction rituals. No more of this craziness.

But her resolve never lasted for long. If she stayed away from men, Roxanne would find herself gravitating to the office lunchroom where her coworkers followed the daily soap operas. If she avoided the television, she would pore over the lurid novels that beckoned to her from the drugstore bookshelves. She endlessly replayed the scenes she read about, picturing herself as the heroine, floating through exotic lands, swept off her feet by handsome strangers.

The "fix" provided by soap operas and novels was a pale substitute for the real thing. Invariably she would return to the hunt for a living, breathing male who would respond to her advances and give her the sensations she craved.

Romance addicts seek what they cannot have because they cannot face what they really want.

Roxanne was addicted to romance just as surely as any alcoholic is addicted to his bottle. There are millions of women like her—women whose energy flows and whose senses are heightened only when they are swept up in the intoxication of a romantic relationship. They seek what they cannot have because they cannot face what they really want.

Nicholas's Story

Women are not the only ones who suffer from romance addiction. Nicholas was 39 years old and had been married for 12 years. He had never strayed from his wife. Indeed, he could never remember a time when he had even been seriously tempted. His wife was a delightful woman, talented, attractive and full of energy. Nicholas would have classified his marriage as excellent, especially compared to many of his friends who complained of dull, unappealing wives and relationships gone stale. Nicholas could point to no significant problems in his marriage.

Nevertheless, Nicholas noticed a growing restlessness. The closer he got to his fortieth birthday, the more restless he became. His job was unfulfilling—surprisingly so, since it represented the attainment of everything he thought he had wanted. He had aimed for the top of the organization, but now that he was there, Nicholas took no pleasure in looking down at those who worked under him. Most of them were intimidated by him; he felt more and more isolated. The pursuit of success had left him little time to develop close friends away from the office.

Nicholas would often daydream about leaving it all behind. He envisioned himself walking out the door one morning and, instead of heading for the office, boarding a jet bound for some remote Mediterranean island. He would not be alone, of course. He pictured beautiful, exotic women who would cater to his every whim.

This fantasy developed as time went on. Nicholas mentally selected the wines he would drink and the choice foods he would eat. He fancied himself becoming an artist and sculptor. The more dreary the daily grind became, the more vivid and detailed his dream became.

One evening Nicholas and his wife were in a restaurant and Nicholas struck up a conversation with the waitress. She was young and vivacious with blonde hair and lively blue eyes. As the evening wore on, Nicholas became more and more focused on her. He was virtually oblivious to his wife's conversation. In his mind, he was on his Greek island—only this time he was there with the blonde waitress.

This was the first time his fantasy had featured a real person. Previously he had populated his dream world with only imaginary women. But the blonde waitress now seemed an integral part of the scene. Nicholas and his wife finished their meal and went home. He went away strangely stimulated, but also strangely disturbed. For the first time in his life it occurred to him that he was not really as satisfied with his wife as he had thought. That night he made love to her with greater passion than normal. But in his mind he was not with his wife at all—he was on a Greek island with a woman whose name he did not even know.

He woke up the next morning with a knot in his stomach. At first he could not pinpoint the source of his discomfort. There was a numbness, a vague sense of guilt and a feeling of distance from his wife. Then he thought back to the night before. It was the first time he had ever fantasized about another woman while making love with his wife, the first time he had ever let his escapist dream take on such a concrete, personalized dimension.

In all but the most literal, physical sense, he had been unfaithful to his wife. The thought slowly formed in his mind: *Was this just a one-time slip or the beginning of a gradual drifting away from his once-secure existence?*

Work was uneventful that morning, but Nicholas still had trouble concentrating. His mind kept wandering to a remote island, to the blonde stranger, to disturbing memories of making love to his wife while picturing another woman. He could not get the waitress out of his mind. The more he struggled to concentrate on his work, the more he thought of her. He wondered who she was, where she lived, what she was like.

Nicholas decided he needed a break, a change of surroundings. He would knock off early for lunch, drive into the city and take a walk. Then, later, he could return to work with his faculties in better control. But as he pulled out of the parking lot, his thoughts were still on the blonde waitress. He wondered what she did when she was not working. He somehow felt certain that if they met, they would discover they had many things in common.

Nicholas circled the downtown area several times, with no particular destination in mind, convinced that he was merely enjoying the ride. Once or twice he drove past the restaurant where he and his wife had eaten the night before, and he glanced furtively in the window to see if he might catch a glimpse of the blonde waitress.

Finally he parked the car and walked to a diner where he often stopped between business appointments for a sandwich and a cup of coffee. As he opened the door, he saw her. It was the woman from the night before, sitting at a table alone, having lunch and, from time to time, scribbling on a yellow legal pad.

Nicholas looked away quickly so she would not know he had spotted her. His heart pounding, he asked the hostess for a table near her. He could see her out of the corner of his eye. Whenever she would look down to work on her yellow pad, he would turn and study her face. She was even prettier than he had remembered.

This went on for about 15 minutes. Adrenaline pumped through his veins as he tried to concentrate on his food. His Greek-island fantasy was overwhelming his mind, flooding him with thoughts about the mysterious blonde, now seated just a few feet away. He struggled with the impulse to talk to her.

Nicholas knew it would be wrong to go further, to flirt and invite danger. But he was drunk on the sensation of forbidden romance—more than he could ever remember being from alcohol. The risk of rejection suddenly seemed a small price to pay in order to find out where the adventure might lead. "Are you a writer?" he asked.

She looked up, startled from her concentration. Yes, she said, she did freelance work for a local newspaper, with an afternoon deadline bearing down on her. She had to finish her story and get it typed before going to her evening job. She worked as a waitress, she said, to make ends meet while she developed her writing career.

Nicholas asked if she remembered him from the night before. She smiled as the recognition dawned on her. Yes, of course she remembered him. Nicholas asked more small-talk questions and she responded with what Nicholas took to be more than mere politeness. He got up from his table and sat across from her. He found her captivating, and she seemed equally interested in him.

After several minutes she said she really had to be going. Nicholas offered her a ride. It would save her time, he said, and help her meet her deadline. She hesitated for a moment and then accepted.

As they arrived at her apartment building she thanked Nicholas for the ride and then stepped out onto the sidewalk. He sat by the curb and watched her go inside. He was almost in a trance. The smell of her perfume lingered in the car, and the seat was still warm where she had been sitting.

He had asked her name. Catherine, she said. Catherine. That was all, no last name. But it was enough. Nicholas felt dizzy. Something had happened, something new and unmistakably real. He had actually made contact with his fantasy. He knew her name, what she did and even where she lived. His pulse was racing as he pulled away from the curb and drove back to work.

As he strode back into his office, Nicholas found that he suddenly felt remarkably calm. There was a peace within him, as if all his turmoil had mysteriously disappeared. With the peace came a kind of euphoria, almost a giddiness.

The sensation surprised him. There had been no physical contact at all, no affair, nothing. He had simply met a friendly person and given her a lift. How could a chance meeting, so insignificant, so innocent, make him feel this way? Nicholas felt calm, excited, out of control and on top of the world, all at the same time. He attacked the mountain of paperwork that had accumulated with gusto.

That evening, as he drove home from work, he found that images of his wife and images of Catherine were somehow blending together in his mind. Who did he hope to see when he got home? Who did he expect to greet him? As he drove, the car seemed to be drawn, almost apart from his having anything to do with it, toward the restaurant where Catherine worked. Nicholas drove past slowly and caught a glimpse of her through the window.

A sensation like the one he had felt at noon stirred briefly, but only for a moment. Reality suddenly came crowding in. He had a wife at home, a wonderful wife, whom he loved and who loved him. She had done nothing to deserve being treated this way by her husband.

On the other hand, why shouldn't he be able to be friendly with someone like Catherine? For 12 years he had been the model of faithfulness. Surely that was enough to justify one innocent, platonic relationship with one other person.

Nicholas had no desire to run off with Catherine. His marriage and his family were in no way jeopardized. Everyone had dreams and fantasies, didn't they? And everyone had casual acquaintances of the opposite sex, didn't they? He wasn't doing anything so different or so wrong. Besides, he was under so much stress. Where was the harm?

At the same time, as innocent as he knew this new experience to be, Nicholas realized that it was something he could never share with his wife. This was something new, something unprecedented. Until now he had never felt the need to conceal anything.

To be sure, there were aspects of his life his wife didn't understand, or wasn't interested in, especially work-related matters. They seldom talked about such things. But this was different. His wife would no doubt be quite interested, even appalled, to learn that her husband had developed a crush on another woman. But she must never know.

Besides, the more he thought about it, the more he realized just how troubled his marriage really was. His wife was not without her faults, after all. In the past he had been able to overlook them, but they were still there. She was so unresponsive at times! No wonder he was drawn—no, driven—to someone else.

Who could blame him? What had his wife done, after all, to keep the romance in their relationship? How could a normal, healthy male be expected to stay excited by a wife who did so little to keep the excitement alive? Certainly he would never consciously do anything to hurt her. But if she found the idea of his having a female acquaintance painful, she had no one but herself to blame.

That night, tossing and turning in bed, the gravity of what he had done hit Nicholas with awful force. Good Lord! He had been with a woman who was not his wife. He had pursued her—jumped in his car and gone out looking for her! She had been in his car. He had actually been to her apartment. Nothing had "happened," of course, but still.

Remorse engulfed him like a flood. How would he feel if his wife had done the same thing? He would be furious. None of the clever rationalizations he had recited that afternoon would make one bit of difference.

How could so much happen in less than 24 hours? Last night he had never seen this Catherine, never even thought about anyone like her. Now she was a part of his life. He had met someone else in the last 24 hours, too—a Nicholas he never imagined existed, a Nicholas whose existence shocked him.

His confusion turned to panic as he wondered whether any traces of his new experience had been evident to his wife. Surely something that made him feel so different would make him look and act different, perhaps in ways he could not control, could not hide. Surely his wife would notice something about him, something new and strange and different. Maybe she had already noticed it, was already guessing at what had happened.

The sense of shame overwhelmed him. What was he going to do? Should he tell his wife what was going on? Would bringing it into the open free him from the attraction or intensify it as the truth drove his wife further away? Where was this experience headed? Was this really just a fleeting occurrence that would soon pass away and be forgotten? Or had he unknowingly, unintentionally, set himself on a course that would end in the destruction of his marriage?

Nicholas wanted to stop thinking about Catherine, but her image would not leave his imagination. He wanted to know her better, but he didn't want to be untrue to his wife. His stomach felt as though it were tied in knots. He felt trapped. Hooked. And he could see no way to get free. Even as he resolved, over and over again, to have no more to do with Catherine, his mind invented new ways of running into her "by accident," and flooded his imagination with images of what might be.

No. This was wrong. He was a married man. A happily married man. A happily married Christian man who had meant what he said when he took his marriage vows, and who was old enough to know better than to let an absurd infatuation destroy everything he believed in and held dear. It was over. He would no longer go to the restaurant where Catherine worked. He would never again drive past it. Someday he would tell his wife all about it and they would have a good laugh. It was over, and it would never happen again. Next time he saw someone who captured his fancy, he would turn away. He would be more loving to his wife, more attentive to her needs. It was over.

But it wasn't over. Nicholas did not end his romantic adventure with a spate of promises from a sleepless bed. No sooner had he awakened the next morning than the obsession returned. He was barely able to complete the day at work. He came home "the long way," cruising past the restaurant where Catherine worked, hoping to catch sight of her. But she wasn't there.

To make up for the high he would have gotten from seeing her, Nicholas dropped into a local lounge and ordered a double scotch. By the time he had finished it, he had run through the entire cycle of shame and despair, and was again making gallant promises to put an end to this ridiculous obsession.

Nicholas didn't keep those promises, however. He pursued Catherine until at last he captured her affection. He had no intention of having a sexual relationship with her. He just wanted to see her sitting across the table from him or next to him in the car, and know the thrill of a fantasy come to life. He had found a high he thought only teenagers could experience.

On occasion his wife would go out of town and Nicholas would be able to spend hours with Catherine, lavishing on her the attention he no longer desired to give his wife. His heart raced when he was with Catherine and seemed to die when he was at home with his wife.

He knew, of course, that what he was doing was wrong. Even though the relationship was not sexual, it was still destroying his marriage. At regular intervals, as the cycle played itself out, Nicholas longed to pull back from the edge of the precipice. But he didn't know how.

When Catherine finally landed a career-track job and moved away, it was a major setback. A deep depression came over Nicholas. His heart ached for her. There seemed to be no relief. He would daydream for hours of the times Catherine and he had spent together—just as he once had fantasized about his mythical Greek-island paradise. Sometimes he would go to places where they had been together and just sit there, trying to recapture the lost moments.

Nicholas longed to pull back from the edge of the precipice. But he didn't know how.

Then one day he was in a shop buying sunglasses when he struck up a conversation with an attractive woman customer. She seemed friendly and interested in him. Before they knew it they had chatted for more than an hour. They both had to hurry back to work but agreed to meet that evening for a drink.

Nicholas was walking on air the whole afternoon, and that night he slept better than he had since Catherine left. In his dreams, he was on an exotic island in the Mediterranean, being served fine wine and choice foods by the lovely woman he had met that afternoon in the store.

An Addiction with Many Forms

Nicholas, like Roxanne, was a classic romance addict. He was hooked on the intoxication of romantic fantasy. For both Nicholas and Roxanne, the central focus was attraction. The answer to all their problems was to retreat into a fantasy world of forbidden romance. All they needed was someone to play the role of the other partner.

Nicholas and Roxanne fed their addictions with relationships with real people. But romance addiction can take other forms, both in men and in women. Many do not involve other people at all. Some romance addicts are hooked on novels or soap operas. Others become fixated on the picture of a total stranger—a model in a magazine or catalog, for instance. Some use pornography, not for sexual gratification but for romantic stimulation. Still others need no outside source of stimulation at all but are content with retreating into their own inner fantasy world.

Some romance addicts focus their attention on celebrities, people they have no hope of ever meeting. They can fall into a deep romantic involvement through contrived fantasies in which the celebrity sweeps them off their feet and carries them away. In some cases these addicts cross the line into neurotic obsession, including attempts to contact or even harm the celebrity. Items such as pictures, autographs and articles of clothing become, in the mind of the romance addict, "proofs" of the reality of the relationship even though they have never met the object of their fascination.

Inevitably, romance addiction, like any other addiction, begins to interfere with the addict's life. What once brought relief soon brings pain, demanding more relief, causing more pain and so on. What was once a technique for control takes control and throws the addict's life out of balance. The addict cannot work or play without the obsession rearing its head. He or she may spend huge sums of money on books or videos, or on attempts to make contact with the object of their obsession. Everything else in life takes second place to feeding the addictive craving for romantic intoxication.

Ironically, in almost every case, the true object of the obsession is not another person, whether real or imagined, but the addict himself. The addict is totally focused on his or her own broken soul, filled with the hurts caused by people who have abandoned him or her in the past. Only one thing matters: feeling better now. Only one thing is sought: immediate relief from pain.

Little attention or concern is wasted on anyone else. It is almost impossible for romance addicts, in the throes of their obsessive thinking and behavior, to see beyond the shell of their own self-absorption to the pain they cause others. All they know is that they hurt, and that they must have what they need to salve their wound. If in the process they wound another, then that is unfortunate, but it cannot be helped. Getting the romantic "fix" is all that matters.

The Pursuit of an Illusion

For the addict, the pursuit of romance is the pursuit of an illusion, one that grows dimmer and more elusive with each failed attempt to erase the pain. The addict becomes involved in a never-ending quest to manufacture a "moment" that will last forever. It never does, of course. It is like drinking from a cup that is riddled with holes; the satisfaction is gone by the time the cup reaches the lips. The mythical handsome prince who will banish all pain and disappointment never comes. The perfect love of a beautiful woman never materializes.

But to the addict, the object of his or her desire seems to be always on the horizon, around the next corner, in the face of each new acquaintance. Their true love will suddenly appear and in an instant everything will be "perfect." There will be no need for the usual arduous process of relationship building: getting to know one another, learning one another's thoughts, plans and dreams, sharing experiences. No, there will be instant love, instant gratification, love and joy and freedom from the hurt, all "in the twinkling of an eye."

The focus of attention is not on the other person as a person, but as the depersonalized embodiment of a fantasy. There is no thought of the nature, the character or the core of the partner, only of the external appearance, the outward charm, the mood, the setting and the "magic."

The illusion seems unslayable. No matter how many times a romance addict has been through the cycle before, no matter how many times those impossible dreams have been dashed, the certitude persists that this time it will be different. The whirlwind of infatuation negates all painful reality—until the addict hits bottom yet again, crushed and bewildered by the disappointment of impossible expectations.

Running from Intimacy

Romance addicts believe they have greater needs for intimacy than other people. Caught up in a cycle of acting out their addiction, they believe they are achieving that intimacy—even if in objective reality they are doing nothing more than watching a movie, surfing the Web or reading a paperback book. They would describe themselves as romantic and sensuous, full of passion and driven by love.

Yet romance addicts are entirely without intimacy. Not only do they not have it, they actually hide from it. Everything they do that seems to be reaching out for intimacy is in fact turning away from it. Their need to be in control prevents them from being intimate with anyone but themselves. In the name of seeking the genuine treasure of intimacy, they settle for fake pearls of false romance and ersatz love.

Romance addicts dream of love, self-esteem and nurturing. They conjure up feelings of intimacy that produce a temporary and illusory sense of wholeness. But genuine intimacy involves risk: disclosing one's inner heart and emotions, and making oneself vulnerable. For this risk of vulnerability, the addict substitutes the cheap thrills of the hunt, of escaping detection, in pursuit of the fix.

Taking Hostages

Romance addicts are love terrorists who take their lovers hostage. They bind them with syrupy words of flattery and with manipulation that has been raised to an art form. They appear to be motivated by a desire to find someone they can care for. It is only when the victim has been taken prisoner that their motive is exposed as self-serving and destructive.

The victims awaken to find themselves trapped in a relationship that robs them of freedom and dignity. They will be used, and when they have been used up, they will be discarded. It is like diving into a river of emotion, only to find themselves swept along toward the inevitable waterfall.

Romance addicts are love terrorists who take their lovers hostage.

Romance addicts often display an uncanny ability to keep their hostages bound. They call at just the moment the victim is thinking of getting out of the relationship. They swear fulfillment of their promises of genuine love if only the object of their desire will be patient with them. They isolate the victim's weak spot and exploit it. If the victim never knew tenderness from her father, he provides tenderness. If the victim's father never affirmed him, never told him he was proud of him, she takes on that role. Romance addicts create the appearance of serving the victim—of bending all their energies to make him or her complete—when in fact it is their own needs that are being served.

Searching Without Commitment

Commitment is challenging for everyone. But it is impossible for romance addicts. They go from one heart to the next, searching for the fulfillment they believe they are owed. They desperately crave affection and attention, and they will do anything to obtain it—anything, that is, except make a commitment.

There is always a back door to the relationship, standing slightly ajar, ever available for a quick flight to a new supplier of false hope and superficial attention, and a quick fix for the pain. The addict invests no more than is necessary to grab that momentary gratification. Everything else is saved for the next search.

But once a victim has been selected and pursuit has commenced, the addict will stop at almost nothing to complete the conquest. If the victim shies away, the addict redoubles his or her efforts. If it means granting sexual favors, the romance addict will pay that price—even if, like Roxanne, she dislikes sex. Even if despised, it is nevertheless a tool to be used, a weapon to be deployed.

If the addict needs to go so far as phoning the victim's wife to establish her control, she will do so. In extreme cases, the attraction can even turn fatal if the victim rejects her too forcefully—as in the movie *Fatal Attraction*. The more unobtainable the other person seems to be, the greater becomes the addict's will to win. Yet once having won, the addict will abandon the victim completely. The game is over. It is time to move on to the next round.

Everyone wants romance. Everyone wants to think of himself or herself, and be thought of by others, as a romantic person. Romance is not a bad thing. In the service of a healthy and legitimate relationship, it is wonderful. But for romance addicts, authentic romance in the service of an honest, loving relationship is not the point.

The point is chasing after the hollow images of romance portrayed in the media, in the service of self-gratification. In the addict's desperate search for relief, the addict does not care who he or she hurts. The addict attaches quickly and detaches even more quickly. The addict leaves his or her victims utterly confused as to how something that looked so good and felt so right could end so suddenly and severely.

Romance addicts believe they are searching for love, but without commitment, love is impossible. And romance addicts will use anything but commitment to obtain what they seek.

Romance addicts want only to ease their pain, and romance is their drug of choice. They are as addicted to romance as any drug addict is to the needle or any alcoholic to the bottle. Until they hit bottom and acknowledge their need for recovery, they will continue to hurt themselves and anyone else blind and unlucky enough to cross their path.

The Addiction Cycle

Obsession	Physical or emotional "trigger"
	Consumed by thoughts
	Plots, plans, schemes
	Loss of concentration
	Judgment impaired
The Hunt	Driven to find relief
	Seeks out someone or something
	Point of no return
Recruitment	Movement to resolve pain
	Enlistment, enticement, seduction
	Risk
Gratification	Object of hunt is attained
	Other person steps into desired role
	Thrill of conquest
	Victimization of other party
Return to normal	Feel calm, peaceful
	"Switch" turned off
	Mood altered
Justification	Pain resurfaces
	Rationalizations
	Depersonalization of victim
Blame	Focus on own neglect or abuse
	Refuse to accept responsibility
	Lay problem at another's feet
Shame	Blaming seems inadequate
	Horror at own actions
	What sort of person must I be?
	Stuff feelings
Despair	Elation-depression cycle
	Utter despair
	Resolve to fix what is broken

Promises	"Never again," list of promises
	Fear of breaking promises
	Return to start of cycle

The Addiction Cycle

The phases of the addictive cycle are remarkably easy to see from the outside, but almost impossible to discern from the inside. These phases are, in essence, the same for both Roxanne and Nicholas. As we shall see, they are also the same for those addicted to relationships and to sex.

Obsession

The individual is consumed by thoughts of romantic intrigue. The mind seems to whir away of its own accord, devises plots and plans to obtain the romantic high. Concentration is shattered and judgment impaired. Obsession begins the cycle that drives the individual to the next phase and intensifies as the process plays itself out.

An episode of obsessive thinking can be triggered by almost anything: meeting an attractive person, passing someone on the street, seeing a picture on a billboard, experiencing an emotional low point of self-pity or depression, or even passing through a location where the obsession was triggered on a prior occasion. The very promises the addict makes to avoid triggering the obsession can themselves serve as a trigger. It is truly a no-win situation.

The Hunt

The individual is driven to follow through on the obsession. Inevitably he or she begins to seek out something or someone that will satisfy that drive. If the addict's object of choice is another person, he or she may cruise the singles' bars. If the addict is hooked primarily on novels, movies or the Internet, he or she will often go through rather elaborate rituals of selecting just the right book, video or website, setting the scene with music and dim lighting and so on.

The stronger the obsession, the more diligent the hunt. This is another point at which interference with normal life becomes noticeable: if it results in time away from work or home responsibilities. Only one of two things will stop the hunt: (1) finding the object being sought or (2) being caught looking.

Recruitment

When the object of the hunt is something inanimate, like a book, movie or website, recruitment is as simple as a business transaction: buy the book, rent the video or surf the Web. When the object is another person, however, the recruitment phase is far more complex. Romance addicts become remarkably skillful at enlisting other people to play the necessary role to complete their romantic fantasy. Sometimes this takes the form of a nonsexual seduction.

> Risk only heightens the romantic intoxication.

Recruitment is always risky. The addict might be embarrassed to run into someone he or she knows while buying a book with a lurid cover or renting an unsavory video. Worse yet, the addict might be seen cruising bars or other public places looking for a partner. Worst of all, the addict might find a prospective partner but have his or her overtures rebuked.

Yet that risk only heightens the romantic intoxication. The rush of adrenaline that accompanies the danger of being caught or found out further propels the addictive cycle.

Gratification

Gratification occurs when the addict succeeds, by whatever means, at realizing his or her romantic fantasy. The book, the soap opera, the movie or the website "does the trick." Or the combination of soft music and candlelight enables the addict to play out a Technicolor romantic dream in his or her mind. Or another person is found who responds positively to the addict's advances. The "itch" has been scratched, at least for the moment.

Return to Normal

The immediate effect of gratification is a break in the obsessive thinking—and from the pain that fueled it—and a return to what feels like normal for a little while. The adrenaline rush recedes; the mind seems to clear. The addict feels peaceful.

If it were possible to remain in this state, all might be well. But no one can remain in a state of perpetual bliss and freedom from stress. Inevitably, the pressures of real life build up again, and something triggers a new round of obsession, hunt, recruitment and gratification.

Justification

The very fact of having "resolved" these problems by resorting to romantic fantasy or acting out frequently brings its own feelings of guilt and remorse. The addict then begins to justify his or her behavior. The addict convinces himself or herself that what he or she did "wasn't so bad," that "everyone does it," that it was "normal" or at least "understandable" for someone with unique circumstances and special needs. The addict's self-talk sounds like this: "But I needed it. I deserved it. Besides, I really had no choice. It's just the way I am. I was only doing what comes naturally to me."

In this phase particularly, the addict rationalizes what he or she has done to the victim. Even if the gratification involved another living, breathing, feeling human being, the addict depersonalizes the entire episode. In the addict's mind the other person was not a real person at all, just a component in the staging of a complex romantic drama.

Blame

Most addicts cannot successfully rationalize their behavior without blaming someone for it. Addicts will blame their parents, spouse or someone from their past who has let them down, and then lay their underlying pain at their feet. Fundamentally, addicts refuse to take responsibility for their own situation, but instead blame others for "driving" them to make the choices they make.

Shame

Justifying and blame-shifting only go so far. Invariably the addict carries a residual awareness of what he or she has done—and of what his or her actions say about what kind of person he or she must be. Inevitably that awareness comes to the surface in the form of guilt over what the addict has done and shame over who he or she really is.

The very nature of shame is that it be repressed—"stuffed" deep inside the addict's mind and heart, rather than brought into the light and dealt with. Thus the addict sows deep seeds of self-loathing—seeds that will eventually give birth to the pain that launches the whole cycle all over again.

Despair

The experience of careening from high excitement at the outset of the cycle to shame and guilt at its conclusion, and the awareness that the cycle is unstoppable, produces hopelessness. When the fix is off, the addict's whole world comes crashing down. The sense of pain or emptiness that originally fueled the addictive behavior is nothing compared to the agonies of depression and despair. And those agonies get worse with every trip through the cycle.

Promises

Because the pain is so great, the addict swears "never to do it again." The addict will be different. The addict will think differently. The addict will live a new life. The addict will never go to "those places" or read "those books" or watch "those movies" again. Yet the prospect of keeping all these promises—the same ones the addict has made, and promptly broken, so many times before—only heightens the sense of frustration and adds to his or her despair. The addict knows it is only a matter of time until the obsessive thoughts start to crowd in again, when he or she will be caught in the addictive cycle once more.

CHAPTER 3

Hooked on Relationships

Mary Jane's mother committed suicide when Mary Jane was 11 years old. Like any young child in such a situation, she believed that her mother's death was her fault; that if she were a very good girl, God would bring her mother back. Mary Jane tried every way she could to attract God's attention by her good deeds. Day after day passed, but God refused to bring her mother back. The depression that had set in after her mother's death grew steadily worse.

Not that Mary Jane and her mother had been all that close. Her mother was a hard woman to get close to, so wrapped up in her own problems that she had little time or energy for anyone else.

Her extreme mood swings were very confusing to her young daughter. One day, she might whisk Mary Jane off to the store and buy her hundreds of dollars worth of new clothes. It was great fun, whirling through the stores, picking out whatever she wanted. Mary Jane remembered how full of life her mother was on those days. She seemed energized, indomitable. At such times, Mary Jane herself could seemingly do no wrong. She was her mother's little princess.

But the excitement of those occasions was tempered by the awareness of what was sure to happen next. A day or two after one of the "good days," Mary Jane would find her mother still in bed at noon, crying, complaining of a terrible headache. Mary Jane always felt so helpless at these times. She wanted to do something, anything. She wanted to fix her mother, take away her pain, make her "okay" again.

Mary Jane would run to her own room and cry, pleading with God to help her mother. Her prayers never seemed to be answered. For days, her mother would mope around the house, the only evidence of life being her occasional outbursts of rage. On those days, Mary Jane could do nothing right. At the least provocation, her mother would lash out at her, sometimes hitting her and sometimes shaking or even choking her.

Even the terror of those awful days did not destroy Mary Jane's feelings for her mother. She still loved her and still wanted to do something to make her problems go away. But her mother's suicide extinguished all hope of that.

Several months later, just as Mary Jane was starting to adapt to the loss of her mother, a new woman arrived on the scene. One of the accountants in her father's office had befriended him after the loss of his wife; they had grown close in the months since.

Her name was Sabrina. When her father started bringing Sabrina home, it was confusing and distressing to Mary Jane. She couldn't understand how her father could be interested in anyone besides her mother. Even more, she couldn't understand how her father could be interested in someone besides herself. She felt intense jealousy toward Sabrina from the beginning. She spent as little time as possible in her presence and would have avoided her entirely if she could.

For her part, Sabrina tried hard to win Mary Jane over. She brought her presents, talked to her and tried to do things with her. But Mary Jane deflected her attentions at every turn, and Sabrina soon came to recognize the distaste the little girl had for her.

Mary Jane's father either did not notice the problem or was too emotionally damaged to try to do anything about it. Once a strong, self-reliant man, he had become weak and wimpy, distraught over the loss of his wife and easily manipulated by the new woman in his life. Whatever Sabrina wanted, Sabrina got. Mary Jane's father seemed relieved that there was someone else willing to take responsibility for his life.

The worse her relationship with Sabrina grew, the less interaction Mary Jane had with her father. He seemed to feel that he had found the answer to his problems and was not about to let anything or anyone interfere with it. Sabrina quickly picked up on this and abandoned her efforts to befriend Mary Jane. Instead, she began to find ways to punish Mary Jane for her lack of allegiance.

Less than three months after Sabrina's first appearance at the house, she and Mary Jane's father were married. Mary Jane was horrified at the thought that this hateful woman would now be living with them. She sought every opportunity she could find to be away from home, leaving for school early and coming home late.

One night, she came home a little too late. It was almost seven o'clock, long after the dinner dishes had been dried and put away. The minute Mary Jane walked through the door, Sabrina grabbed her by the arm and angrily dragged her off to her room. She took a coat hanger from the closet and began beating Mary Jane relentlessly. The girl screamed but her father did nothing to intervene. She was forced to stay in her room for two days without food. She had to sneak out to get water and use the bathroom. It was the beginning of two years of torture for Mary Jane.

The physical abuse and the virtual imprisonment became more frequent and more severe. Mary Jane thought about God during these times. She was convinced He must hate her if, indeed, He existed at all. Or maybe she was the problem. She had caused her mother's suicide, so now she was bringing this punishment upon herself. She felt terrible shame at being such a bad person.

Mary Jane's father was no help. She tried to approach him more than once, but he would not connect with her emotionally, let alone offer any help. He seemed prepared to sacrifice his daughter for the sake of surrendering responsibility for his life to his wife.

Mary Jane wanted to escape, to leave the nightmare behind. She tried to run away a couple of times, but she always got caught and had to come back—and when she did, the beatings and deprivations at the hands of her stepmother were worse than ever. Finally, when Mary Jane was 14, she left for school one morning but went to the police station instead. She told the officer at the desk that she wanted to report someone for child abuse.

Mary Jane was removed from her home and placed in a girls' school. Her father agreed to pay for her expenses. She felt intensely alone and isolated. Her mother was gone. Her father had traded her in for an angry, controlling stepmother who was worse than any evil fairy tale stepmother. She felt empty. Mary Jane desperately wanted relief from her pain, and she soon found a way to get it.

> **Mary Jane learned to invest whatever was necessary to keep a new relationship going. She was willing to pay any price, even if the price was her own identity.**

About a mile down the road was a boys' school. Once a month on Saturday nights, a dance was held which brought the two schools together. At first, Mary Jane found these events uncomfortable. She was extremely shy. But behind the timid veneer, she couldn't wait to attract the attention of a boy. Before long, she would go to the dances and attach herself to one of the boys as quickly as possible and not let go for the remainder of the evening. During the following weeks, there would be letters, phone calls and attempts to plan a weekend rendezvous.

Mary Jane felt desperate to keep her boyfriends interested in her. It soon became evident that this was going to entail sex. She surrendered her virginity to the first boy who asked for it. She was 14 years old.

Male attention was soothing to her ravaged soul. Just hearing someone tell her he loved her was enough to send her into ecstasy. To be touched and caressed gave her sensations of security and peace she had not known since her mother's "good days" so many years before. Mary Jane disliked intercourse but was willing to tolerate it if that was the price for keeping a boy's attention. She learned to invest whatever was necessary to keep a new relationship going. She was willing to pay any price, even if the price was her own identity.

All of Mary Jane's relationships were strictly a one-way street. What mattered were her desires, her needs. The boy's role in the relationship was to fulfill the role of emotional provider. She began each new alliance with the hope that this would be "the one," that special relationship that would wipe away her lifetime of misery and abandonment. But that magic cure-all connection never seemed to appear.

The longer her search continued, the more desperate she became, and the more unappetizing her candidates became. Soon, Mary Jane would hook up with anyone who would give her the attention she craved and a momentary taste of the security she sought.

The downward spiral seemed to come to a halt when Mary Jane went to college. It was there that she met Kevin. He was a senior, a football player and a fraternity member, and he seemed willing to give Mary Jane all the attention she wanted. He saw in her someone who would not threaten his intellectual limitations or question his authority.

When he was drafted by a pro-football team, Kevin insisted that she leave school and marry him. Mary Jane did so gladly, envisioning a life of emotional and financial security. With his salary and bonuses, financial success came easily.

However, in other respects, their life resembled a master-slave relationship more than a marriage. All Kevin wanted was someone to clean the house, keep the kids out of his hair and fetch him a beer when he was thirsty. Mary Jane gave it her best. Outwardly, she seemed to have it all. Inwardly, she was miserable because of the lie she was living and the unmet needs she still carried.

But Mary Jane never complained. She hung in, ever the loyal wife, through her husband's rise to fame and his subsequent fall into obscurity. Released from the team and unequipped for any other way of earning a livelihood, he did poorly in business. Soon, they had lost everything. Kevin's anger—always channeled onto the playing field when he was in sports—now found expression at home. He started drinking heavily as well and became increasingly abusive toward Mary Jane and their three children.

Still, she did not complain. She never demanded that Kevin seek help, never threatened to leave. Mary Jane could not conceive of life without him. She convinced herself that he needed her, that only she could love him back to health and stability. She made up her mind to fix him, no matter what it took.

She stood by her decision without wavering for more than two years and might never have departed from it had it not been for a chance meeting in a neighborhood convenience store. It had been a long day and her emotional tank was running low. She had stopped to pick up a gallon of milk for the kids' breakfast the next day.

Standing in line at the checkout counter, Mary Jane got into a conversation with a nice-looking older man buying a magazine. He seemed keenly interested in her and very understanding of her frazzled condition. They continued talking as they walked out to the parking lot. By the time they reached their cars, Mary Jane had agreed to meet him for lunch.

The exhilarating experience of being wanted by someone—after so many years of being merely tolerated by her husband—seemed to unleash something deep inside. The desire to attach herself to someone else had been squelched for so many years. Now that it had been released, Mary Jane wasted no time. Within a week, she had left home and moved in with the man she had met in the store. She no longer cared what happened to her husband or her children. Mary Jane was free at last, or so it seemed—free to devote her energies to someone who at last could meet her needs and fulfill the inner void.

However, the cycle repeated itself with dismaying regularity and rapidity. What at first seemed like freedom soon came to feel like captivity, and Mary Jane would once again break loose from one relationship only to throw herself into another. By the time her fiftieth birthday arrived, Mary Jane had lived with 10 men and been married to six of them. Each time she was sure that "this was the one." Each time she was bitterly disappointed.

Turning 50 was a pivotal point in her life. There had been so many hurts, so many disillusionments—surely there had to be a better way. Perhaps it was not too late to change. Mary Jane finally allowed herself to seek help. As she embarked on the painful process of resolving her past so she could live at peace in the present, she was finally able to obtain what she had sought after so long and so fruitlessly.

Addicted to Attachment

As with any addict, Mary Jane felt a great deal of pain. There was a wound to be healed, an ache to be soothed, a void to be filled. But rather than turn to drugs or reach for a bottle, Mary Jane sought relief in relationships.

Relationship addiction is different from romance addiction. Rather than getting hooked on the intoxication of a romantic experience, the relationship addict is hooked on the attachment to another person who has responded to him or her with attention. It is the *attachment*—the sense of belonging, of being needed—that is paramount. There need be no romance, no soft music, no candlelight. Sex need not be involved.

The attention paid by the other person need not even be of a positive nature, as long as it is *there*. An addict will prefer to remain in a destructive relationship, preferring the pain of physical abuse to the terror of abandonment. As with any other addiction, it is *progressive*. In other words, it gets worse, not better, as time goes on. The addict jettisons all concepts of self-worth and personal dignity. Keeping the attachment—or finding a new one—is all that counts.

Relationship addiction is dismayingly easy to feed in a society like ours, a society filled with empty and broken hearts desperately longing to be made whole. The addict has little trouble finding someone to attach to. There are millions of hurting people eager to swap their freedom and dignity for a modicum of relief.

That relief, of course, usually comes in the form of control. Relationship addiction combines "underresponsible" and "overresponsible" people in an unholy alliance of mutual dysfunction. One wants to dominate, the other wants to be dominated. Neither has trouble finding a suitable complement in our lovesick culture.

Addiction or Codependency?

Codependency is an increasingly familiar concept in our culture. A codependent is someone who becomes locked in a relationship with a dysfunctional person in such a way that he or she becomes dysfunctional. Every addictive or compulsive problem produces its own form of codependency in spouses, children, friends, coworkers—anyone who is in a close relationship with the afflicted individual.

The classic case is the alcoholic's wife. She adjusts her perceptions and adapts her behaviors to accommodate the craziness caused by his addiction—all the while denying that the problem exists. In the end, she becomes just as sick as he is, though in her own distinct way.

Many people who read Mary Jane's story would conclude that she is a classic codependent: growing up with a manic-depressive mother skewed her perception of what is normal in human life and relationships, and made her grow to be a dysfunctional person in her own right. And, indeed, Mary Jane was a classic codependent. She constantly and neurotically tried to fix others, blindly sacrificing her own welfare in the process.

But there is more to Mary Jane than merely being codependent. Codependency is a disorder of attachment, but it typically focuses on a particular person, usually on someone who is a fixture in the codependent's life. Parents and spouses are the most common culprits.

Relationship addiction is also a disorder of attachment, but it focuses on an endless series of people previously unconnected to the addict. Many of the behaviors are similar, but the object of the attachment is different.

Mary Jane was both a codependent and a relationship addict. During her childhood, and again during her first marriage, she was codependent with her mother and later with her husband. At other times, she exhibited the distinguishing traits of the relationship addict, going from one relationship to another in search of the one attachment that would make everything okay.

Roots of Relationship Addiction

At the root of relationship addiction is the unspoken but unshakable conviction: "No one could ever love me just for who I am. They will love me only for what I do, only if I work hard and prove myself competent at what they consider important."

Usually, a foundational rejection early in life convinces the addict that he or she will inevitably be rejected again and again—unless the addict does something to prevent it. As a result, the relationship addict, powered by a full set of "Try-Hard" batteries, erects systems of perfectionist behavior in a futile attempt to earn love and acceptance.

At heart, the problem is *fear*. Fear of rejection. Fear of abandonment. Fear of not measuring up. This fear colors everything the addict does.

Ironically, the addict cannot succeed in relationships with emotionally healthy people precisely because they are healthy. Healthy people are strong enough to see the addict's problems and to leave when those problems begin to manifest themselves. Thus, healthy people actually pose a threat to an addict—the threat of abandonment. It is dangerous to establish relationships with emotionally healthy people, because they are almost certain to leave and trigger the anguish of abandonment all over again. As a defense against this possibility, the relationship addict most often attaches to a weak and dysfunctional person.

At heart, the problem is *fear*. Fear of rejection. Fear of abandonment. Fear of not measuring up. This fear colors everything the addict does. The addict becomes insecure and apprehensive about everything. If he or she does not attach to someone else, the addict fears he or she will be unable to survive. Once the addict does attach, he or she is driven by the fear of abandonment into patterns of behavior that virtually ensure the dismantling of the relationship. Thus, the cycle is created: The addict can do nothing but go from one unhealthy relationship to another.

Rejection early in life exacts a high price later on. It leaves the person with an almost insatiable thirst for approval. Men rejected by their fathers find themselves uncomfortable with their manhood, not certain what is expected of them, not certain what it means to be a man. Similarly, women who experience early parental rejection grow up confused about their womanhood.

Our culture's ambivalence about how women are supposed to behave doesn't help matters any. It is okay for a woman to be assertive, but not pushy. She can sacrifice for another out of love, but must take care not to become codependent. The never-ending drive for approval from others, based on living up to societal expectations, is frustrating—and, for the relationship addict, devastating.

Seeking external affirmation in this way is like living on a raft in the middle of a storm at sea. You are constantly being thrown this way and that by the waves of other people's expectations. More often than not, the shell of who you are stays afloat while the real you sinks to the bottom. You lose touch with your own needs and wants, and instead focus on others. You try to control them in a misdirected effort to calm your own storm-tossed inner life. Other people appear as life preservers floating on the surface of the waves. Only by attaching yourself to them can you hope to keep your head above water.

Rose-Colored Glasses

One root of the relationship addict's behavior is that he or she wears rose-colored glasses that make each new acquaintance look like the perfect candidate for this kind of life-preserving attachment. There is no such thing as objectivity; the addict is driven to over-glamorize. Deflated by low self-esteem, the relationship addict assumes that everyone else *must* be superior. Any units of weakness or imperfection that may appear on the surface are ignored. Even glaring deficiencies are overlooked in the overwhelming need for emotional rescue.

Once the addict has attached, it is almost impossible to let go of the relationship. The addict has already told his or her friends how wonderful the new person in his or her life is. Even as those with eyes to see question how long it will be until the new relationship turns sour, like all those that have come before, the addict vigorously assures them—and himself or herself—that this one is *different*. The addict's emotional investment is so strong, and the addict's need to save face so great, that he or she hangs on for dear life.

In time, the rose-colored glasses that a relationship addict wore at the outset turn into the dark glasses of *denial*. The addict denies the obvious weaknesses and deficiencies of the other person. The addict also denies the reality of his or her own glaring problems. The addict denies the signs—unmistakable to everyone else—that this relationship, too, is headed for a dead end.

What Others See and Think

- "I think she should just leave him."
- "You know, he has someone on the side."
- "Why does she always end up with someone who treats her so badly?"
- "Can't he read the handwriting on the wall?"
- "He treats her like dirt."
- "She's like a magnet that attracts all the flakes of the world."
- "What is it about him that makes him stay married to a woman like that?"
- "Why does she keep going from one loser to another?"

Anger

Anger is another root of relationship addiction. Relationship addicts are among the angriest people you will ever meet—and often they aren't even aware of it. Beneath the friendly smile and pleasant disposition displayed to the world lies a seething cauldron of boiling emotions—resentment over the past; rage over the present. The addict goes to great lengths to keep this anger bottled up, knowing—often at a subconscious level—that to let it out would be disastrous.

The addict also seeks to suppress the expression of anger in other people as well. In the addict's emotional memory bank, anger is associated with rejection and abandonment; therefore, it must never be allowed to appear under any circumstances. The addict becomes the ultimate people-pleaser, working overtime never to give offense, never to do anything that might occasion an outburst. The turmoil generated by squelching the addict's legitimate needs in order to avoid antagonizing others only feeds the bottled anger that fuels his or her addiction.

When Someone Is Angry, the Addict Believes It Means:

· They hate you.
· They are going to reject and abandon you.
· You must have done something wrong to make them feel this way.
· You are a bad person and should feel ashamed of yourself.

The Guilt Magnet

While the relationship addict runs from anger, he or she clings to guilt. The addict is apologetic about anything that goes wrong for anyone, whether or not he or she had anything to do with it.

This trait is very appealing to under-responsible people. They have been searching all their lives for someone who is willing to take the rap for the mistakes they have made and the problems they have caused. Such people are attracted to relationship addicts like iron filings to a magnet.

This extreme guilt is actually a fruit of self-obsession. The addict is constantly focusing on *my* problems, *my* failings, *my* weaknesses, the mistakes *I* have made. The perfectionist-performance mentality the addict has adopted for himself or herself feeds into this. The addict sets standards that he or she cannot possibly meet; then, when the addict falls short, he or she blames himself or herself and sees his or her short-comings as the cause of everyone else's problems. Thus, the addict's apparent focus on the needs of others is, in reality, a twisted way of focusing on self.

The other reason why relationship addicts typically struggle with guilt is the inadequate foundation of self-esteem laid in childhood. As I have already noted, early emotional or physical abandonment is a common denominator among relationship addicts. There is a void in their lives where there should have been appreciation for God-given talents and personal accomplishments.

Guilt and fear rush in to fill that void. Therapists know that the overwhelming majority of children of alcoholics, drug addicts, divorced parents and so on feel personally responsible for their parents' problems. At some level, they are convinced that they, the children, were the cause. Most transfer that self-directed guilty verdict to all of their future relationships.

Relationship Addicts and Sex Addicts

Frequently the wandering relationship addict meets up with a wandering sex addict. Together they form the perfect symbiotic relationship, each one feeding on the other's problem. Sex addicts are the perfect candidates for relationship addicts, because they typically have so much guilt and shame for which they need someone else to take responsibility. And as we have seen, taking on responsibility for others' problems is the relationship addict's stock in trade. Sex addicts so desperately need this psychological "out" that they will never leave—making the perfect nonabandoning partner.

This is not to deny that there can be elements of authentic love in such relationships, of warmth and genuine concern for each other's needs, but frequently the basis of the relationship is more problematic. Sex addicts are often practiced seducers, and the relationship addict can mistake their polished seduction for the "magic" of romance. Also, there is always the need, on the part of the relationship addicts, to "fix" their partners and to protect themselves from abandonment.

Curiously, relationship addicts do not view their partner's sexual adventures as abandonment, only as signs of a problem they are sure they can help repair. I once spoke to a female recovering sex addict who had recently shared with her husband some details of her sexual life she was sure he knew nothing about. In fact, he did know about them and had known for some time.

Why had he never said anything? She was his fourth wife, and he was so afraid of seeing yet another marriage collapse that he could not bear to confront her. Besides, he assumed that with his sorry marital track record, his wife's wanderings had to be his own fault. In short, after some probing and reflection, it became evident that he had the classic symptoms of relationship addiction.

In a relationship like this, while the sex addict rides the roller coaster of sexual adventure, the relationship addict hangs on for dear life. He or she hangs on as long as it appears that hanging on will prevent another round of rejection and abandonment. The relationship addict would rather be in a miserable relationship than in no relationship at all.

Why Relationship Addicts Stay with Sex Addicts

- Love
- Magic
- Challenge
- It's all they think they deserve
- The good times, when they occur, seem great
- To "fix" or "save" the other person
- Even a bad relationship is better than none

Characteristics of a Relationship Addict

Relationship addicts live in a world of paradoxes that leaves them feeling they have no way out. They desperately want to get close to someone, but end up with a person whose problems make closeness impossible. They seek security, but end up with someone who always leaves the back door open for a quick getaway.

Relationship addicts crave unconditional love, but live in constant fear of abandonment if they don't live up to their own impossible standards. They want to be free to love, but often trap themselves in a relationship by becoming pregnant or by weaving some other type of emotional spiderweb. Drowning in the whirlpool of their own emotions, they turn to a rescuer who cannot swim.

Many common characteristics can be found in people who suffer from this form of addiction.

Experience early deprivation. Relationship addicts were often rejected or abandoned in childhood, and may well have been the victims of physical or psychological abuse.

Feel unloved or rejected by the world. Viewing life through the lens of their own painful experience, addicts assume that the world is just one big dysfunctional family.

Are insecure. Addicts are full of fear and doubt, overwhelmed by the stresses of daily living. The only way they see to survive is to attach themselves to someone else.

Attempt to earn love. Relationship addicts become perfectionists toward themselves, setting standards they can never hope to attain. They believe they have to be "good enough" to be loved by another.

Attempt to "fix" others. Relationship addicts try repeatedly to "fix" others, usually persons who do not want to be fixed. The drive to save someone causes the addict to hang onto a relationship long after others would have left.

Attract very needy people. Anyone with an obvious need or deficiency becomes a magnet: the needier they are, the less likely they will be to walk away. Also, the needier they are, the more likely they need fixing.

Attract abusive or emotionally distant people. Addicts are often attracted to people cut from the same mold as their own parents, often in an attempt to symbolically win the parents' favor and love. By the same token, addicts are often uncomfortable around healthy people who might be strong enough to live without them.

Move quickly from attraction to attachment. Addicts "latch on" to someone with remarkable speed, in hopes of cementing a relationship.

Determine to keep the relationship going. It may be a disastrous and destructive relationship, but it seems better to addicts than no relationship at all. As long as it is still alive, there remains hope that it may improve.

Lack whole, healthy people in their lives. The roster of past relationships and acquaintances is filled almost exclusively with damaged and needy people, in contrast to whom the addict can appear healthy and normal.

Walk on eggshells. Relationship addicts are afraid of rocking the boat. They are excruciatingly cautious about everything they do in an effort to avoid the wrath of others.

Appear to be meeting others' needs first. In fact, everything addicts do, even the things that look the most sacrificial, are done to meet their own need to be loved and needed. They appear unselfish, but are in fact willing to let another person spend a lifetime in distress if it guarantees their role as "fixer."

Fail to recognize their own needs. Relationship addicts are unable to see the selfishness of their own motives. They may believe they need to be more assertive, when in fact what they need is to resolve their own selfish need to be needed.

Burst out in rage. Relationship addicts try to keep their anger bottled up, but they cannot do so forever. Sooner or later their pent-up anger explodes. Such outbursts are followed by periods of deep remorse and attempts to make things right again—to forestall the dreaded abandonment.

Never ask for help. Rather than seek help, addicts prefer to battle their problems alone. They cannot risk being found out, which allows someone else to discern the true nature and extent of their problems.

Feel uncomfortable if others do things for them. This only causes the addict more guilt and greater fear of not "measuring up."

Do not have hope of ever finding a truly loving relationship. Early childhood experience has convinced them that it will never happen.

Possess inordinate patience. Addicts astonish their friends by their ability to "hang in" for years without the faintest glimmer of hope for change in their destructive relationship.

Are euphoric at the start of any new relationship. Relationship addicts constantly assure themselves and others that this time is going to be different. Overblown hopes and expectations are attached to each new prospect.

Feel responsible for all problems. Addicts assess everything that happens in terms of their own efforts. If anything goes wrong, it must have been their fault.

Defend against everything. Addicts place so much performance pressure on themselves that they are resentful of perceived attempts to add more.

Feel inadequate. Relationship addicts never look right, weigh the right amount or say the right things. They find it impossible to live up to their own expectations.

Alienate themselves from others. Addicts feel like outcasts—as if everyone else but them has been given the manual on how to make human life work.

Crave affirmation. Addicts draw what little self-esteem they have from the sense that they are trying hard and doing a good job. They feast on others' comments about how loyal and patient they are.

Despise sex. Sex is only a means to an end, not a source of joy and pleasure in its own right. It is to be endured, never enjoyed, if that is the price to maintain the relationship.

Exert control. Addicts will seek out needy people whom they are able to manipulate and dominate. They may appear to be subservient to a domineering spouse. In reality, however, it is they who have the upper hand.

Search for happiness. Relationship addicts are martyrs. They so accustom themselves to the apparently hopeless pursuit of happiness that they actually resist finding it.

Manipulate. Addicts will invest extraordinary amounts of time and energy determining what patterns of behavior will produce the desired effects in other people. They learn how to elicit attention, how to elicit affection and even how to elicit anger.

Are frequently depressed. Because of their past rejection and abandonment, relationship addicts have few emotional resources to draw on in times of stress. Instead, they simply shut down.

Express multiple compulsive behaviors. The emotional turmoil that accompanies relationship addiction cannot lie dormant. Frequently, it finds expression in other problems such as compulsive overeating, spending or gambling. These compulsive behavior patterns become increasingly intertwined.

Doubt. Relationship addicts are plagued by insecurity and are never sure of themselves. They constantly vacillate in even the most routine decisions.

See themselves and others as victims. If their partner is a sex addict, it is because others have deviously seduced their partner. If their partner is an alcoholic, it is because of the stress others have placed him or her under.

Compensate. Relationship addicts try to compensate for what they did not have as a child by manipulating others to get what they want. They compensate for weakness by acting strong. They compensate for selfishness by creating the appearance of selflessness.

Mind read. Since the way to find acceptance is to please others and meet their expectations, addicts engage in a never-ending mind game: What does someone else really want? To come right out and ask would be to tip their hand.

Get angry over unmet needs. Addicts never express their own needs. Indeed, they may be largely unaware of them, but they go through life with a vague sense of being "ripped off."

The Addiction Cycle

Obsession	Self-focus
	Hurts from the past
	Feelings of abandonment
	Negative emotional state
The Hunt	Looking for love in all the wrong places
	An available victim
	Well-rehearsed ritual of enticement
Recruitment	Tricks of the trade

	Submissive nature
	Mating calls
Gratification	New energy
	Solving another person's problems
	New attachment
	Instant feeling of relief
Return to normal	A new companion
	Feeling of completeness
Justification	I needed it
	I deserve it
	I had no choice
Blame	Usually focused on parents first
	Spreads to others
Shame	Self-pity
	Recognizes attachment to the "wrong person"
	Self-betrayal
Despair	Feeling trapped
	Overresponsibility
Promises	"Never again!"
	Focus returns to hurt and pain
	Obsession restarts addictive cycle

The Addiction Cycle

The stages of relationship addiction parallel those of romance addiction. The motivation, the process and the results are all the same. The only difference is the source of the gratification. The romance addict is hooked on attraction, while the relationship addict is hooked on attachment. The addiction cycle again begins with obsession.

Obsession

The relationship addict is fixated on self. The addict constantly relives past hurts and develops a "you owe me" attitude toward the world around him or her. Obsessive thinking leads to compulsive behavior, as the negative emotions fueled by the obsession drive the addict to find some form of relief, some source of positive mood alteration.

The Hunt

As the obsession grows, the addict starts "looking for love in all the wrong places." The search is on for someone to whom an attachment can be forged. Over time, this phase can become a full-blown ritual, as the addict develops a well-practiced repertoire of attitudes and behaviors that have proven effective in the past.

> Fear, guilt and depression all lift at the prospect of a new someone to live for. The new attachment suddenly appears in the addict's mind as *exactly* what he or she was looking for.

Recruitment

Many techniques are used to recruit a partner/victim. Flattery is effective when the target is someone with a weak or bruised ego. An outward display of submissiveness can also be used: Addicts talk about how tired they are of "running the whole show" or how they wish they could just hang it all up, settle down and take care of someone else for a change. These and many others constitute the "mating call" of relationship addicts seeking attachment.

Gratification

In the days following the initial contact, as the target shows signs of interest and even suggests the possibility of attachment, the addict enjoys new energy. Fear, guilt and depression all lift at the prospect of a new someone to live for. The new attachment suddenly appears in the addict's mind as *exactly* what he or she was looking for. For the first time, the addict feels free and peaceful and whole—for the first time since the last time, that is.

Return to Normal

For a while, the relationship addict feels "okay" about himself or herself. With a companion safely at the addict's side, the world no longer seems like such a terrifying place. The addict feels complete. But the superficiality of the relationship soon starts to appear through the thin veneer of good feelings, and the addict begins the downward spiral to reality.

Justification

As addicts feel the pain starting to creep back in, they try to justify the fundamental dishonesty they used in seeking out their victim; the addicts try to justify why they stayed so long with someone so sick. Addicts tell themselves they need to feel okay. They persuade themselves that they deserve it because they work so hard. Addicts convince themselves they *had* to do it—justify the repeating of mistakes that have led to such heartache so many times before—or their world would collapse.

Blame

As the addict allows reality to sink in regarding how unhealthy the relationship is, the addict begins to blame others for his or her problems. Astonishingly, even when the addict's new partner disappoints his or her expectations, or even worse, becomes emotionally or physically abusive, the addict still looks for someone else to take the blame. More than likely, the addict starts with his or her parents. Before long, the addict will have turned on anyone and everyone who has shown himself or herself less than 100 percent successful at fulfilling his or her expectations.

Shame

Blame soon turns to shame as the addict realizes what he or she has done and is doing. The addict realizes, however fleetingly, that he or she has, once again, become attached to someone who cannot live up to his or her expectations. The addict realizes that the whole process is a selfish exercise designed to rid himself or herself of pain.

The pain that drove the addict into the process in the first place returns, only now it is compounded by the shame of seeing his or her own actions. The addict sees that he or she has betrayed others, but the addict has also betrayed himself or herself, selling out his or her principles for the sake of hanging on to yet another hopeless relationship.

Despair

Guilt from the past combines with shame from the present to produce deep hopelessness. Addicts find themselves caught in a trap of their own making. Addicts want out of the relationship but dare not leave because of the consequences, both to themselves—*my world will collapse*—and to their partner—*but who will take care of her if I'm not around?* The many "I told you so's" they hear from friends and family only compound their sense of despair.

Stooping So Low

· Doing things you don't want to do
· Doing things you promised yourself you'd never do again
· Staying with someone who treats you badly
· Never bringing yourself to say no

Promises

Addicts swear that if they can just get free from their current mess, they will never again latch on to another loser. Addicts promise themselves over and over that this will be "the last time." They promise themselves that they will seek help. Addicts also promise themselves they'll never go into a singles' bar again.

The very fact of making these promises only focuses their attention on their guilt and shame, and the pain only drives them into the addictive cycle all over again. Until the root pain from the addicts past is resolved, and their focus is transferred from themselves to others, they will remain trapped in the downward spiral.

Perhaps more than with any other addictive problem, the things relationship addicts do seem utterly senseless to those around them. They are so overwhelmed by past hurts and self-obsession that their ability to make decisions becomes impaired. They will fight to stay in relationships even when they are abusive. They will look for new relationships in dangerous places. In order to establish or maintain a relationship, they will do things they have promised themselves never to do again. They will stay with someone who humiliates them in front of others. They will refuse to say no to their partner even at the cost of their dignity.

Relationship addicts practice "smother love." They seek someone to "fix" and then smother them with attention in an effort to block out their own pain. In so doing, they surreptitiously manipulate their partner, controlling the relationship to avoid their own greatest fear: being abandoned yet again. Yet in smothering their partner, they smother their own soul. They also smother their relationship with God as they try to earn their way into a phony heaven of their own devising.

When addicts find a likely partner, they fling their half a soul at that person in hopes that the attachment will make them whole. But because most partners are themselves as wounded as the addict, what they get back is a soul more damaged than they started with.

The resulting feelings of hopelessness drive many relationship addicts into other addictions such as drugs, alcohol or overeating. In the meantime, they hang on desperately to a death-dealing situation, convinced that even a disastrously bad relationship is better than none at all.

Relationship addicts find themselves trying to fix the whole world, one relationship at a time. Each time will be the last time, they tell themselves, because each time they are convinced: "This is the one that will work." Or in the case of a codependent who returns again and again to the same destructive relationship: "This time it will be different."

Finally, relationship addicts come to the end of their own strength and need to seek God in order to resolve the hurts of the past and help them focus authentically on the needs of others. Apart from such a spiritual intervention and a move toward a genuine focus on others, relationship addicts are doomed to a cycle of misery and futility. They can never fix what only God can fix. They must recognize that it is in the depths of their own broken hearts that God wants to begin the process of recovery. (See appendix A to assess whether you may have a relationship addiction.)

CHAPTER 4

Hooked on Sex

Mark traces his sex addiction to a day not long after his eleventh birthday—the day he discovered masturbation.

Life in Mark's household was tense. His father was a corporate executive who was as emotionally distant when he was home as he was physically distant during his frequent business trips. His mother found it increasingly difficult to deal with the stress of raising a family on her own. Mark sometimes came home at the end of the school day to find her mysteriously calm, her gaze distant, her speech dreamy. It was only in later years that he learned to associate these episodes with the bottle of tranquilizers she kept hidden in the top drawer of her night table.

His father's frequent absences as well as his mother's escapism meant that a large share of the responsibility for keeping the house together—getting his younger brother off to school in the morning and getting dinner served and the dishes cleaned up—fell on his shoulders. Sympathetic neighbors commented on how lucky his parents were to have a son like Mark.

Mark didn't feel lucky, however. He felt burdened and anxious. Whenever he could, he would retreat to his bedroom and bury himself in the stack of comic books he had been collecting since childhood. He would spend hours spinning fantasies in his mind about the characters in the comic books, placing himself at the center of their adventures, imagining himself interacting with them.

In particular, he imagined himself with the women characters that populated the stories. Their exaggerated figures, exotic costumes and glamorous looks riveted his attention. He pictured himself saving them from the various dangers portrayed in the stories as they gazed at him with gratitude and admiration. It sent a rush of excitement through him, picturing himself not as a dutiful 11-year-old boy whose mother did not appreciate him, but as a brave and accomplished warrior whose exploits made beautiful women swoon.

It was while he was lost in just such a reverie that Mark experienced his first erection—and a few moments later, his first ejaculation. He was terrified. Nothing like this had ever happened before. There must be something wrong. But who could he tell? The experience was confusing and embarrassing. And, to make matters worse, it felt good in a way that nothing had ever felt good before. Even as he lay there, frightened about what had happened, he found himself wanting it to happen again.

In the days that followed, *wanting* it to happen turned into *making* it happen. His comic-book fantasies increasingly became preludes to masturbation. Mark had furtively searched through a health textbook in the school library and reassured himself that what he was doing was normal, if not entirely acceptable. So he kept his new experience to himself. He found it a very effective means of getting his mind off the stresses of living at home. His fantasies were not primarily romantic or sexual in nature. Masturbation merely helped heighten the sense of excitement that washed over him during his adventurous daydreams.

But as time went on he more and more clearly tied his masturbation to images of women—not just the cartoon characters in his comic books, but any pictures of women. Seeing a pretty girl in a magazine or in a catalog or on television—especially if she were scantily dressed—would trigger a desire for the momentary but intense "high" that masturbation produced.

By the time he was in high school, Mark indulged that desire daily, sometimes several times a day. By now he had developed a virtual encyclopedia of mental images to dwell on while masturbating. Sometimes they were drawn from pictures he had seen. Occasionally they were based on real people: girls in his classes, women he saw in stores. But they were always embellished and enhanced in his mind—no longer real individuals at all, but fantasy women whose purpose was simply to energize his solitary sexual encounters.

It wasn't hard to graduate to pornography. Some of his friends had managed to swipe copies of the more popular men's magazines from local drugstores or from their fathers' closets. Mark soon established his own source of supply: a friend of his father's who kept a large stash of such magazines hidden in his basement. He looked forward to visits to this man's house. Invariably Mark would manage to leave with three or four copies of the magazines hidden away. His collection of comic books gave way to his new collection of skin magazines.

Each new discovery, each new level of explicitness, only seemed to heighten Mark's thirst for more.

His fascination with the women in the magazines seemed to supplant his interest in girls. Mark dated occasionally, but found little excitement in it. He was nice looking, athletic and could have been reasonably popular. But taking a girl to a basketball game or a school dance didn't give him the rush of adrenaline he got from the women in his magazines.

Going away to college at long last delivered him from the emptiness and drudgery of family life. It also gave him the freedom to explore whole new worlds of pornography, worlds he had heard about but had never dared to investigate. Some of the bookstores near campus sold magazines and paperback novels that went far beyond anything he had encountered before. He would spend hours browsing their racks, thumbing through the magazines and books, feverishly looking for "the good parts." Then, armed with new, raw material, he would go back to the dorm and spin out Technicolor fantasies while he masturbated.

But it never seemed to be enough. Each new discovery, each new level of explicitness, only seemed to heighten his thirst for more. One day he cut classes and took a bus to the downtown section of a nearby city. There, in a rundown street, was a theater that advertised "XXX-rated" films.

He had seen the ads for these films in the newspaper many times and had frequently thought of going to see one. But now that he was actually there, standing across the street reading the lurid titles on the marquee, he felt frightened and excited all at the same time. What would it be like inside? What if someone saw him go in? What would he *really* see on the screen?

He felt dizzy as he crossed the street and entered the theater—as if it were not really he who was doing it, as if he were somehow above or outside himself, watching it happen. He asked the man at the ticket booth what time the next show started. The man didn't answer. He just rolled his eyes and slid Mark's ticket through the slot in the window. Mark took a deep breath and went inside.

What he saw took his breath away. There on the screen, bigger than life and in shocking full color, were a man and woman actually doing things—right there, right in front of him—that he had only read and dreamed about.

He felt as though a line had been crossed, as though he had done something that could never be undone. It was as though this new experience had catapulted him to a higher level of stimulation, and he somehow knew he could never again be satisfied with what he had known before. Magazines and books wouldn't be enough anymore. He would have to have this experience again.

The sensations Mark experienced that day were to become familiar to him as the years went on: the giddy anticipation of a new adventure, the strange detached feeling as he embarked on it, the dizzying sense of crossing a line from which there was no crossing back, the hot shame at the realization of what he had done.

Mark's addiction to pornography was able to thrive apart from the rest of his life. It seemed to have a life of its own, apart from who he was and what he did. He remembered the characters from his childhood comic books who would step into a telephone booth and suddenly emerge in an entirely new identity.

It was like that for Mark. Much of the time he lived a seemingly normal life: going to class, studying, horsing around with his friends. Then he would figuratively step into a booth and emerge as his alter ego, avidly poring over books and magazines, slipping away to the movie house—or simply into his well-stocked imagination—for an afternoon of sexual fantasy.

In his "normal" mode, Mark finished college and took a job. He also got engaged to a girl he had known in school. She was bright and attractive and devoted to Mark. She was utterly unlike the women who populated his fantasies. Mark saw his relationship with her as being totally separate from his "other" life. Indeed, he had persuaded himself that marriage would mark the death of his "other" self, that a regular sex life with a woman who loved him would take away the need, and thus the desire, for pornography and masturbation.

He was shocked to find out how wrong he was. His resolve to put pornography and masturbation behind him lasted less than two weeks after the honeymoon. He had wrapped up a business appointment unexpectedly early and was headed home—as it happened, through a part of town where one of his favorite adult theaters was located. The car seemed to steer itself along the familiar route. Almost before he knew what was happening, Mark was inside the theater. He made sure he left in time to get home at the usual hour. His wife never suspected a thing.

Mark felt sick. He had been sure that marriage would eliminate his drive for "outside" sexual stimulation, but it didn't. The "other Mark"—the one that couldn't stay away from porn—hadn't disappeared after all. He still lived, and he still expected to have his appetites sated.

Mark discovered something else unexpected. The impulse for pornography and masturbation was *different* than the impulse for sexual intercourse with his wife. He would have thought that being with his wife would satisfy the desire for pornography. But it didn't work that way. It was as though they were two entirely separate appetites. Satisfying one did nothing to satisfy the other.

His wife was attractive and anything but unresponsive in bed, but the urge to go to an X-rated show could come over him even the morning after they had enjoyed satisfying sex. Less than a month after his wedding day, Mark was back into the pattern of porn use and masturbation that had characterized his life as a bachelor. It was only a matter of time until the next line was crossed.

Mark's job took him on frequent out-of-town trips. He had long since learned how to satisfy his cravings for sexual fantasy while on the road—the world of business travel seemed specially designed for people like him. Airport bookstores sold magazines and hotel rooms offered late-night adult movies. No big city was without the special shops that offered "peep shows," where for a quarter you could watch a brief snippet of an X-rated movie.

In some cities the peep shows featured live women dancing in the nude. Mark found these establishments distasteful. He was afraid of the kind of people he might encounter there. But in time his curiosity got the better of him, and he started frequenting them. He learned which shops he enjoyed the most in each city and began to visit them whenever he was in town.

It was during an especially long out-of-town trip that Mark crossed a major line for the first time. His company had sent him for a two-week training seminar. During that time he lived in a downtown hotel room. He was the only person from his company attending the seminar. Some evenings he would join other participants for dinner. One night he went out to a movie with one of the men. But most nights he wound up in his room, alone and lonely.

Next to the telephone was a directory of entertainment options in the city. He had thumbed through it idly while calling home. His attention kept focusing on an ad for an escort service. It was primly worded, as though it were offering refined, college-educated women to accompany executives for black-tie business dinners. But the sketch of the voluptuous woman that accompanied the ad suggested that something more than polite dinner conversation was available.

Mark picked up the phone and then put it back down at least a half-dozen times before he finally dialed the number. His heart pounded as he listened to the phone ring. The adrenaline was really flowing. Who would answer? What would they say? What would *he* say? Finally he heard a click and a bored-sounding female voice on the other end recite the name of the service and ask, "How can I help you?"

Mark quickly and carefully placed the receiver back in the cradle. He felt like he was going to faint. What a rush! He had never really intended to follow through—for a man like him to actually place a phone call and order up a prostitute was, well, it was ridiculous. Pornography was one thing, but to do something like *that*—but the sheer excitement of it was literally breathtaking.

Mark sat down on the side of the bed. He felt dizzy. He was far too keyed-up now to just turn on the television and go to bed. He slipped his jacket on and went out. The hotel had a cocktail lounge—a drab affair with dim lights and old, worn chairs around small round tables. Mark didn't drink. But tonight was a night for adventure. He sat down at the bar and ordered a whiskey.

He was so flustered by the mysteries of ordering a drink, and still so distracted from his phone call, that he didn't even notice when a woman sat down at the stool next to him. She smiled and said hello. He nodded dumbly and smiled back. She seemed to be about his age, nicely dressed—probably a business person like himself in town for meetings or a seminar. She asked what he did for a living, and he told her. Then he told her about the seminar he was taking. She was a sales rep for a manufacturing firm, she said, in town for a trade show. She smiled again. She seemed nice.

Mark's head was swimming. It was all too much: the phone call, the whiskey and now the new intoxication of talking to this attractive woman. The strange but familiar sensation came back, of standing outside himself, watching what was happening. From his "outside" perspective he seemed to know what was coming. He wasn't sure he wanted it to happen, but there didn't seem to be any way to stop it. It was as though it were *supposed* to happen.

When he tried to tell himself to stop, to get up and walk away, his body simply refused to respond. Part of him knew he ought to leave. But the "other" part of him wanted to stay—wanted to see where this new adventure would lead, as if this were some sort of special opportunity that might never come his way again. He couldn't pass it up.

And he didn't. The woman made some vague comment about hating "places like this," and Mark mumbled agreement. She suggested they go to her room, and he agreed again. He was really on fire now; whatever chance there had been of turning back was gone.

He awoke in his own room the next morning as if from a bizarre dream. The furtive phone call, the bar, the drink—and the sudden, sickening realization that he had actually been sexual with a strange woman. He lay back on the bed, feeling literally sick.

What had happened? How had it happened? Surely it couldn't have happened to him? He tried to think it through logically—even tried to pray about it—but he couldn't pull it all together. He had really crossed a line this time. He felt so ashamed. What was he going to do?

He got up, showered and dressed, and headed off to his seminar. He felt nervous. Surely the other people in the room would know what had happened. They would be looking at him—some with roguish admiration, perhaps, others with disgust. When one of the instructors said good morning to him at the coffee table, Mark flushed and stammered a reply, then hurried to a seat in the back row.

Gradually it dawned on him: no one knew. They had not seen him after all. They were not all looking at him. The seminar went on as if *nothing had happened*. Mark took a deep breath. Maybe it was going to be alright. Last night had been—what? Some strange departure from the norm. An aberration. Nothing had really changed. He was still the same person with the same job, the same wife and the same family. Why had he been so scared? Life went on. *Nothing had really changed.*

When the two-week seminar ended, Mark went back home. He put the adultery behind him, or so he thought—as though he could just get on a plane and leave "all that" behind. But he couldn't get the woman out of his mind. As dazed and detached as he had felt at the time, he found he was now able to relive the experience with total emotional recall. He would suddenly "come to" while sitting at his desk and realize that he had been daydreaming about that night, replaying it over and over in his mind. Not merely replaying it, but embellishing it with a seemingly endless series of erotic variations: things he had done, things he *wished* he had done, things he would do next time.

> # The question was not so much whether there would be a next time but *when* would be the next time.

Next time. The very arrival of the thought, unplanned, unbidden, made him catch his breath. Would there really be a next time? And then: of course there would. How could there not be? Crossing the line had been so effortless, so easy. And *nothing had really changed.* Life had gone on as before. His wife hadn't noticed, any more than she had ever noticed the magazines or the books he kept so well hidden, any more than she had noticed the masturbation he never said anything about. The question was not so much whether there would be a next time but *when* would be the next time.

His new responsibilities at work, for which the seminar had prepared him, soon began to take their toll. There was more money, of course, and a nicer office and greater prestige, but there was also more stress and longer hours. He frequently worked through dinner, not getting home until late, long after his wife had put the kids to bed, often after she herself had gone to bed.

Mark dealt with the loneliness and stress the way he always had. His visits to the downtown adult bookstores became more frequent. Often he would drop by after hours, on his way home at night. One of the stores was part of a nightclub that featured loud music and nude dancers. He never went into the nightclub section, as a rule. He didn't usually have time for it; it was quicker just to browse the magazines and check out the peep shows for a few minutes.

But now that his expanded work schedule had made it normal for him to come home late, he had more flexibility. The nightclub gave him an opportunity to practice his newfound pastime of drinking—you *had* to order drinks, it was a rule—and besides, there was a thrill in watching a real, live woman that you just didn't get from staring at a photograph in a magazine or watching a videotaped image on a television screen.

It didn't take him long to learn the ropes: how to get one of the dancers to come to your table and perform, just for you; how to arrange to meet her later in one of the private "lovers booths" that the club provided; how large a "tip" was considered appropriate for the various services that were available.

His visits to the nightclub became more and more frequent and began eating into the rest of his life more and more as well. Occasional visits after hours were no longer enough. Now he would slip out during lunch, sometimes not returning to the office for hours. He was coming home late several times a week. After a while he started to run out of excuses and explanations for the frequent absences.

His wife stopped asking him where he'd been. Mark assumed she had simply adjusted to his new schedule; he didn't realize how patently absurd some of his explanations had become and that she had stopped asking him to avoid the pain of being lied to so obviously.

Work was a different matter, however. His boss knew what Mark's schedule was, or at least what it was supposed to be, and he knew Mark wasn't keeping to it. He knew of the long absences, the weak explanations, the liquor on Mark's breath when he came in. He also knew of the charges of sexual harassment from women in the office who complained of the leering glances and remarks Mark would cast in their direction when he thought no one was listening. Mark's boss called him on the carpet on several occasions and warned him what would happen unless he changed. Mark would express regret and promise to do better.

And he would, for a few days. But then the obsessive thoughts would come again, until he couldn't concentrate on his work any longer. He would manufacture an excuse to go out, and then head for the nightclub or one of the so-called massage parlors downtown. On more than one occasion Mark was so desperate he picked up prostitutes off the street in broad daylight. It was no big deal, he told himself. Guys did it all the time. He could cover things back at work. He always had.

Mark's downhill slide was accelerating. His boss finally had no choice but to let him go. That was a shock, but Mark brushed it off. The company never *had* acknowledged his true abilities. Armed with a positive recommendation from his last boss, who felt bad enough about firing him and didn't want to make life worse for him, Mark was able to find a new job fairly quickly.

It was during the physical exam required by his new employer that Mark learned he had contracted chlamydia, a common venereal disease. That, too, was a shock. But again Mark brushed it off. Other people had worse sicknesses; he wasn't going to die; no one needed to know. That he might have been responsible for spreading the disease to others—including his wife—never seemed to occur to him.

The night he finally woke up was the night he came home to an empty house. His wife and children were gone. The note she left behind pointedly refused to say where they had gone; she didn't want him to be able to locate them. She expressed hope that he would seek help for his problem, whatever it was (she had an idea but wasn't sure), and that he could find a way to turn his life around. But he would have to do it without her. She was gone from his life for good.

Mark poured a drink and fished one of his pornographic videos out of its hiding place. When he turned the TV on, the channel was set to a religious station. Mark and his wife were churchgoers, and though Mark didn't consider himself especially devout, his wife had been taking a greater interest in church lately. He sat down to watch the program for a minute. Should be good for a few laughs.

The program was about sex addiction. Mark felt uncomfortable but couldn't stop watching. The man being interviewed was about his age, and his story sounded eerily like Mark's. Mark suddenly felt angry. He was no sex addict! He felt like cursing the man on the screen. But as he watched and listened, his anger turned to profound grief and he began to cry.

When a phone number came on the screen for a local treatment center, his heart skipped a beat. Mark picked up the phone and put it back down at least a half-dozen times before he finally dialed the number. His heart pounded as he listened to the phone ring. The adrenaline was really flowing. Who would answer? What would they say? What would *he* say? Finally he heard a click and a voice on the other end recited the name of the center and asked, "How can I help you?"

Can Sex Really Be Addictive?

Could the behavior Mark found so difficult to stop be more than just a moral weakness? Was his downward spiral inevitable? Was there any lasting answer to the anger and grief Mark felt when confronted by the reality of his condition? Can sex really be addictive?

The experience of countless others seems to support this conclusion:

· A husband and father of three children fears that if he continues to have sex with other men, he will become infected with the AIDS virus. His wife has already contracted genital herpes as a result of his lust for men. He does not want to die of AIDS. But every time business takes him out of town, he ends up having sex with one or two men he has never met before. He cannot understand why he cannot stop.

· A widow, at the suggestion of a friend, buys a vibrator to increase her arousal during masturbation. When she uses it, the pain of her loneliness eases. But she still feels guilty. This kind of behavior is not normal or proper for a lady like her. Still, her use of the vibrator continues until one night she causes physical damage to herself. She has to have a friend drive her to the emergency room to get the bleeding stopped. She is humiliated. She is also frightened at her inability to quit.

· A father hears his eight-year-old daughter and her friends playing downstairs. It is the beginning of the slumber party he has been fearing all week. He tries to stop himself, but soon takes his usual place outside the living room window, peering into his own house, spying on the young girls in their pajamas. As he is masturbating, a neighbor spots him and shines a flashlight on him. His face flushes as he tries to explain, mumbling something about the stress he has been under. The neighbor, shocked and confused, says and does nothing.

For these three people, as for Mark and thousands—perhaps millions—of others, sex has become a drug. Like any drug, it is used in an attempt to deaden pain: the pain of rejection, loneliness, fear, anxiety, childhood abuse or any of a dozen other hurts.

But it doesn't work. Sex masks the pain for a moment, providing a brief mood change. The short-lived relief comes not just from the orgasm, but also the ritual leading up to it—the seeking, which becomes the central organizing factor of daily life. But in the long run, instead of making the pain better, it ends up making it worse as the person experiences deepening humiliation and loss of control over his or her life.

Sex as an Addictive Drug

- It provides a quick mood change.
- It works every time.
- It is used to mask pain.
- The user becomes powerless over it.
- The user loses control as the compulsion takes control.
- Even harmful consequences cannot deter it.

Consider the man who gets through his stressful days by visiting a so-called massage parlor on his lunch hour. The quick and reliable pleasure of the sexual encounter becomes his antidote to the pressures of life. He becomes convinced that he cannot function without this daily "fix." He turns to sex the way a heroin addict reaches for the needle. Until the underlying needs and the emptiness at the core of his life are addressed, his addiction will continue to drive him deeper and deeper into sexual slavery.

The addict becomes powerless to change. Often he *wants* to change and knows he *has* to change, but he cannot do it. Try as he might, some trigger always comes along to set off the obsession yet again. The common denominator of all addictive problems is this: What the addict sought to control comes to control him. Even consequences like the threat of disease, disruption of family life and public humiliation are not powerful enough to extinguish the addiction.

Paradoxes of Sex Addiction

Control

At first, sex seems to be a tool for controlling pain. And, for a while, it "works." The mood change brought on by orgasm kills the pain and provides a momentary sense of being "normal" again, of being "in control." But as the addictive cycle continues, there comes a time when after the relief, the pain returns worse than before, triggering a need for more relief, causing more pain, and soon, until sex controls the individual, not the other way around.

All addictions are built on unrealistic expectations. Alcoholics believe a drink will solve their problems. Overeaters believe that maintaining the "full" feeling will make life better. Sex addicts likewise believe everything will be okay once they get their "fix." That belief cements their determination to obtain it, no matter what. Sex represents—addicts think—the best and only opportunity to bring their out-of-control world back into order. They are like a person who jumps off a skyscraper, thinking everything is under control as he or she passes the twentieth floor.

Rules

Addicts are champion rule makers. An addict's entire life becomes a complicated web of rules that only he or she understands. Who but alcoholics would make the rule, no drinking before noon, and then believe that as long as they didn't drink before noon they were not, after all, alcoholics—not one of *them*?

Elements of Control

· Can't control thoughts
· Can't control behavior
· Can't control spirit
· Can't stop doing what is destroying you
· Believe stopping would destroy you

Sex addicts likewise develop their own set of rules that would be incomprehensible to anyone else. Who but sex addicts would feel the need to establish the rule, never have sex with a stranger, and then reassure themselves that despite having 18 affairs over the course of a year they were not sex addicts—since all of the affairs were with people they knew? But the very making of a rule virtually guarantees that it will be broken. It becomes not so much a boundary line but a goal line to be attained and then surpassed.

Love/Hate Cycle

Sex addiction sets up enormous conflicts in the addict's mind that produce apparently self-contradictory behavior. Sex addicts want help but are afraid of the process of getting better, so they want to be caught even as they work to avoid detection. They lure others into the position of gratifying their desires, and then in anger they repulse and punish them. Unaware of the conflicting drives that motivate their behavior, addicts wonder how the object of their desire can so quickly become the object of their disgust. The frustration is intense.

Parallels to Other Addictions

Sex addiction can readily be seen to have a number of parallels to other, more familiar, forms of addiction.

Addiction is progressive. Like all addictions, sex addiction grows worse over time. It doesn't stand still. The addict does not reach a certain level and then stay there. There is a built-in dynamic that always drives the addict to the next level, and the next and the next. Unless the addict seeks help and makes a commitment to recovery, the end of the spiral is insanity or even death.

Addiction builds tolerance. Alcoholics are notorious for their ability to "hold" enormous quantities of liquor. It is the same with sex: Greater and greater stimulation is required to produce ever-diminishing gratification. The addict has a tolerance for sex that leaves others aghast. Ten sexual experiences a day still leave a sex addict unsatisfied; indeed, the appetite grows stronger, not weaker, with each attempt to satisfy it.

Addiction produces withdrawal. Alcoholics deprived of their bottle get the shakes. Drug addicts deprived of their needle get the "D.T.s" *(delirium tremens).* Gamblers who cannot get to the track, or at least to a phone to call their bookie, become edgy. Likewise, sex addicts suffer withdrawal symptoms when they try, or are compelled, to give up their drug for any length of time.

Addiction follows an obsessive-compulsive pattern. Thoughts of alcohol, or cocaine, or eating, or gambling or sex, begin to crowd everything else out of the addict's mind, until the addict reaches the point where he or she has to do something to make them go away. As the obsession turns to compulsion, sex addicts find themselves in the act of doing things they don't want to do, things they have promised never to do again. It is as though they are standing outside themselves, pleading with themselves not to go on, deaf to their own cries.

Addiction produces shame. In the beginning, sex addicts choose behaviors that are congruent with their sense of what is appropriate. But the force of the addiction eventually drives them into behaviors they themselves abhor. To escape from the burden of shame—which would crush them if they had to bear its full weight—addicts shift the blame for what they do to others.

Marks of Addictive Sex

It is easy to confuse normal sexual desire and conduct with addictive compulsion and gratification. A person can have a stronger-than-normal sexual appetite and not be an addict. Here are some characteristics of addictive sex that help distinguish the two.

Addictive sex is done in isolation. This does not always necessarily mean that it is done while physically alone. Rather, it means that mentally and emotionally the addict is detached, or isolated, from human relationship and contact. The most intimately personal of human behaviors becomes utterly impersonal.

Addictive sex is secretive. In effect, sex addicts develop a double life—practicing masturbation, going to porn shops and massage parlors—all the while hiding what they are doing from others and, in a sense, even from themselves.

Addictive sex is devoid of intimacy. Sex addicts are utterly self-focused. They cannot achieve genuine intimacy because their self-obsession leaves no room for giving to others.

Addictive sex is devoid of relationship. Addictive sex is "mere sex," sex for its own sake, sex divorced from authentic interaction of persons. This is most clear with regard to fantasy, pornography and masturbation. But even with regard to sex involving a partner, the partner is not really a "person" but a cipher, an interchangeable part in an impersonal—almost mechanical—process.

Addictive sex is victimizing. The overwhelming obsession with self-gratification blinds sex addicts to the harmful effects their behavior is having on others, and even on themselves.

Addictive sex ends in despair. When married couples make love, they are more fulfilled for having had the experience. Addictive sex leaves the participants feeling guilty, regretting the experience. Rather than fulfilling them, it leaves them more empty.

Addictive sex is used to escape pain and/or problems. The escapist nature of addictive sex is often one of the clearest indicators that it is present.

Sources and Origins of Sex Addiction

With remarkable consistency, sex addiction finds its origins at the foot of a mountain of childhood abandonment, abuse and family dysfunction. In many cases, it is specifically sexual abuse that launches the addict on a career of abusing others. Some studies estimate that as many as 80 percent of sex addicts may have been sexually abused in childhood. Often the victim grows up to be the victimizer, practicing the behaviors he or she learned from a parent or other significant adult figure.

Of course, not all sex addicts were abused as children. And not all abused children grow up to be sex addicts. Other significant factors also contribute to sex addiction.

Stress Reaction

The initial experiences of addictive sex often occur during times of stress. The person feels trapped and inadequate, and has no one with whom to share the feelings of anger and frustration. Sex provides an escape from this unpleasant reality. The level and frequency of stress can influence how the person progresses along the path of compulsive behavior and then addiction. When stress is relieved, the addiction seems to have lifted. But the individual knows it still lies just below the surface, ready to be triggered by the next set of difficult circumstances.

Operant Conditioning

This is a technical term for the process of easing into the addiction gradually, through repeated exposure to sex and/or to pornography. When stress occurs again, the person resorts again to the pattern of behaviors that provided relief before. This soon becomes a mood-altering ritual that gets locked in place.

The case of Bill illustrates how it works. Bill was raised in a relatively normal home, with no evidence of molestation or other abuse. He describes himself as still being sexually innocent when he went away to college and was exposed to pornography for the first time. His roommate had a subscription to a popular men's magazine, the arrival of which was a major monthly event in the dorm.

In time, Bill discovered masturbation. When he saw the ads in the magazine for "phone sex," he began calling the numbers. His masturbation problem became so severe that he would physically hurt himself. Years later, outwardly a happily married man, Bill's problem remained.

Antipornography activists argue vigorously for the recognition of this as an entryway into sex addiction. They believe that seeing violence or victimization associated with sex leads men to the belief (often unstated, but no less real) that women secretly *want* to be treated violently. After seeing thousands of images, the addict becomes conditioned to become violent anytime something sexual occurs.

Our society helps condition us toward addictive sex. The media have helped make the unusual appear to be the norm—multiple sex partners, repeated affairs, sex on every first date. These behaviors no longer shock the regular viewer of prime-time television. Many who grow up in such an environment will be predisposed to sex addiction even without a history of early childhood abuse or family dysfunction.

Search for Attention

Some contend that a person's most fundamental need is for sex, and for the power to acquire it. I think the greater need is for *attention*. People will do remarkable things to gain attention from others. If they were neglected while young, they may spend a lifetime trying to fill the void left by parental inattention. In the process, many discover that sex seems to provide total, undivided attention.

Such people become hooked on sex, in effect, for the attention it brings. At least for those few moments, someone is noticing them. The withdrawal addicts experience when sex is unavailable is strikingly similar to the childhood depression caused by parental abandonment.

False Beliefs

When sex addicts open up and honestly express their feelings, they say strikingly similar things: "I didn't think I'd ever find someone who would love me"; "I felt unworthy of love or respect"; "I was always convinced I was inadequate"; "The only way I know how to relate to someone is sexually." These false beliefs about self and about the nature of relationships obviously fuel the addictive process.

All of us make choices every day about the kind of life we are going to lead and the kind of person we are going to be. Those choices are based on the foundation of our core beliefs about ourselves and the world around us. If that foundation is faulty, our choices will be faulty, too. The catch is that poor choices reinforce the false beliefs, which in turn prompt more poor choices.

> ## Even if harmful circumstances are helping shape our choices, they are still *our* choices. The path to recovery always involves learning how to take responsibility for those choices.

The Bible states that all people share an inborn propensity to do wrong instead of right, our fallen human nature. Even if harmful circumstances are helping shape our choices, they are still *our* choices. The path to recovery always involves learning how to take responsibility for those choices. But our freedom to make healthy choices is enhanced by our understanding more clearly the factors that influence us, and then taking steps to disarm or counteract them.

Not a Cop-Out

We may find it is easy to criticize the label "sex addiction." There seems to be a fad of labeling every problem an addiction, sometimes in an apparent effort to excuse ourselves from taking appropriate personal responsibility for our actions.

But addiction is no cop-out. Quite the contrary. No addict is absolved of responsibility because he is "sick and can't help himself." Rather, to identify an addiction as such is to enable the person to correctly understand his or her problem so that the person *can* more effectively take responsibility for it. If a person is indeed an addict, failing to recognize and name the problem for what it is will make correcting it far more difficult, if not impossible.

I am convinced that sex addiction is real. In its milder forms, it involves what seems to be relatively innocent compulsive behaviors that harm no one but the individual. But in its more severe forms, it involves serious self-destructive behavior and victimization of others.

Mark, whose story began this chapter, is like thousands of others who know something isn't right, but don't know what to do about it. Men and women, rich and poor, from every racial and ethnic background—anyone—can suffer from sex addiction. Unfortunately, our self-indulgent culture prevents the addiction from being identified early on. Sooner or later, the addict begins to recognize that he or she has a problem. In the case of men, it becomes clear that his sexual behavior is more than that of the "red-blooded American boy."

At some point, the sex addict cannot escape the realization that sex is no longer providing relief; instead, it is building a trap. Desires are out of control as they control the person. Sex addicts do not set out to take on dozens of sex partners or to become compulsive masturbators. They do not seek to abuse or victimize helpless people. They certainly do not intend to ruin their lives and the lives of those near to them. But once the process of sex addiction sets in, the direction of its progression is impossible to predict.

Recovering sex addicts invariably look back in disbelief that they were capable of the behaviors that characterized them at the height of their addiction. They can see clearly in retrospect how much they wanted to be loved and accepted. Seeking relief from the pain of rejection, they betrayed their values, their morals and their very selves. Having been rejected by others, they came to reject themselves over the very behaviors they could not stop. Seeking acceptance, they ended up isolated from everyone.

Levels of Addiction

Like the alcoholic progressing from sipping an occasional beer to guzzling scotch straight from the bottle, like the drug addict graduating from marijuana to crack cocaine, the sex addict inevitably moves beyond his or her current repertoire of behaviors into new forbidden frontiers. Sex addiction, like all addictions, *escalates*.

First, sex addicts fantasize and then look for ways to act on those fantasies. They start, gingerly and tentatively, with mild forms, and then end up plunging headlong into extreme manifestations of the problem. In the beginning, the person has an addiction. In the end, the addiction has *the person*.

In his book *Out of the Shadows,* Patrick Carnes pioneered the idea that sexual addiction occurs at different levels. The following four levels of sex addiction will help you see how addiction progresses.

Level One

Fantasy, pornography and masturbation together constitute the first level of sex addiction. These practices are essentially solitary. They are not considered criminal (except for the more extreme forms of pornography). Society either winks at them as insignificant amusement or encourages them as normal. Yet they form the gateway to deeper levels of enslavement.

Anyone engaged in this first level of sex addiction would have no difficulty justifying his or her actions in light of our society's "liberated" attitudes toward promiscuous sexual behavior. But there is a crucial distinction between the addict and others who are sexually active outside of marriage. Both are doing something harmful and outside of God's will, but those who are not addicted are in control of their actions. Sex addicts are already starting to be controlled *by* their actions.

Fantasy. The first stage of addiction, sexual mind games, seems harmless enough. *What would she look like undressed? Do I have a chance with him? I wonder if she thinks I'm sexy?* These are the kinds of fantasy questions many of us ask at one time or another. But addicts don't just ask them, they obsess over them. They can't stop thinking about them; they can't get them out of their minds. The harder they try to banish these fantasies from their thoughts, the more forcefully they press in on those addicted to sex.

Fantasizing about a trip one hopes to take or meeting someone one admires is healthy, but sexual fantasy involving someone other than one's marriage partner is unhealthy. It offers a pleasurable alternative to an unpleasant current reality; therefore, it occurs most frequently at times of stress or anxiety. Many argue that fantasizing is a normal, healthy part of exploring one's sexuality. This may be true to some degree.

One popular psychologist goes so far as to encourage couples to use fantasy to strengthen their marriage. Fantasy, she says, brings us closer to our partners. This is simply not true. While the world judges by outward appearances, God is concerned with the heart. Jesus said that lusting after a person in one's thoughts is as serious as committing adultery in the flesh (see Matt. 5:28).

Many relationships have been destroyed by fantasy, which can be the first step onto a moving sidewalk away from commitment. Some psychologists say it adds spice to a relationship, but having had a small taste, too many have left the relationship in search of more spice.

> **Pornography is a tool for going beyond reality and beyond the fantasy world that can be constructed by your own imagination. Once used, it is difficult to live without.**

The progression of addiction is primarily a battle for the mind. To stop the progression, the addict must start with the mental battle. Fantasy may seem like a safe, innocent pastime. It is secret. It appears to involve no one else. But fantasy is the opening that allows the addictive process to gain control. The beginning of bringing our will into line with God's plan, with sex as with other areas, is to win the battle for the mind.

Pornography. Fantasy and pornography are closely related links in the sex addiction chain. Pornography is an industry based on fantasy. Here are some of the fantasies that can readily be found in today's pornography: having sex with a small child; having sex while inflicting pain on another; sex as an act of violence; forcing sex on someone and discovering that they enjoy it; having sex with multiple partners at the same time.

Pornography is sold as an emotional getaway car, a vehicle for those who want to escape. It takes the person beyond the boundaries of his or her own limited imagination. When the well of fantasy runs dry, the porn industry is ready with a virtually endless supply of books, magazines, videos and Web sites to help generate new fantasies.

Some realities of pornography seem to stir little concern in its users. For one thing, pornography is a victimizer. It victimizes those who use it, but it also makes victims of those who are used to make it. A lot of money can be made in pornography, and quick money quickly becomes irresistible.

Once involved in the industry, many young people find it hard to wean themselves away from a job where they can make money just by taking off their clothes and acting out someone else's fantasies. They shed their dignity along with their clothing. Their embarrassed families reject them. Those who get into pornography on a lark, or as a "stepping stone" to an acting or modeling career, find their future prospects for career, and even for marriage and personal happiness, permanently stained by their porn past.

The *users* of pornography are also victimized by it. They become dependent on the illusion produced by the stories and pictures. The airbrushed beauty fabricated on the pages of a magazine makes reality that much less satisfying. A man with his mind full of visions of college-age girls finds intimacy with his 50-year-old wife increasingly unexciting. He becomes a victim of his own decision to look at what is not his, what he has no right to see.

A woman who steeps herself in romance novels filled with explicit sex scenes is no less a victim. Through the printed word, she escapes to exotic foreign countries and makes forbidden love to unattainable, idealized men. How will she then be satisfied living with a 45-year-old hus-band who takes her to Niagara Falls in their Winnebago?

Pornography is a tool for going beyond reality and beyond the fan-tasy world that can be constructed by your own imagination. Once used, it is difficult to live without. The sex addicts I have known all got their start with pornography. In fact, serial murderer Ted Bundy, in an inter-view with Dr. James Dobson shortly before Ted's execution in 1989, warned of the dangers of pornography and explained how pornography contributed to the development of his behavior.[1]

Many sex addicts go through a certain progression with their use of pornography. They start with what is usually called "soft-core" porn, the kind of stuff sold in corner drugstores and newsstands—primarily mag-azines with photos of women or men posing alone, in various stages of undress. The thrill fades quickly, however, and they move on to pictures of men and women together.

The next step requires seeking out more unsavory sources like adult bookstores and nightclubs, or explicit depictions, either in print, on video or online of heterosexual or homosexual acts. The next levels may involve pornography depicting sex with children or even animals, and sex involving bondage, simulated violence or the actual inflicting of pain. The final stage is pornography showing people being beaten and strangled, and even mutilated and killed.

Other, less traditional, forms of pornography include: "phone sex," in which a man or woman on the other end will "talk dirty" as long as the caller is willing to keep paying by the minute; strippers that come to people's homes to help them make their own porn movies; and escort services that eliminate the need to cruise seedy neighborhoods looking for prostitutes, because the prostitute is delivered right to the front doorstep.

Masturbation. Despite the incredible variety of forms that porn can take, they all have one thing in common: Pornography is about masturbation. Bluntly put, that is what people do when they use pornography. Porn is not an art form. It is an aid to masturbation. The Playboy mansion was built on the proceeds of men's desire to have sex with themselves while looking at pictures of pretty girls. Freud said that masturbation was the original addiction, and that all other addictions are merely a replacement for it.

Compulsive masturbation, built on fantasy and pornography, is an escape from intimacy. A person who is a compulsive masturbator will be unable to experience genuine intimacy. Sex becomes a one-sided process of self-gratification. The addict would rather masturbate than take the time to develop a relationship. Expecting marriage to eliminate the drive to masturbate, the addict soon finds that intimate sex is too much trouble and returns to the compulsion.

Everyone needs to be nurtured, to feel loved and to feel love toward another. But love is risky. Love holds the possibility of rejection or disappointment. The masturbator finds it easier to fall back on self-gratification. What seems to many like a harmless habit becomes a trap that blocks out others and forces the addict to suffer alone.

Different schools of psychology, and different schools of theology, differ over whether masturbation can be acceptable under various circumstances. But for the sex addict, masturbation is never acceptable under any circumstances.

Level Two

The second level of sex addiction still does not involve criminal behavior, but differs from the first in that contact is made with another person. In level one, the sex was on paper or in the mind. In level two, real live people are involved.

Level two covers everything from going to bars that feature nude dancing to having an affair. It includes fetishes, in which items of clothing or other belongings of a real person become erotic enhancers. It also includes phone sex and all forms of sexual touching that are "accidentally on purpose," such as brushing up against someone in an elevator.

The most common form of level two sex addiction is having repeated affairs. A person who has a fling is not, by virtue of that one instance, a sex addict. But many people whom we now label as simply "unfaithful" could more properly be viewed as sex addicts, since they believe they cannot exist apart from repeated affairs.

The repeated affairs syndrome is just as addictive as heroin or crack. First, there is desire, which leads to perceived need. When the need is not met, sex addicts experience emotional discomfort. Finally, they find relief through consummating the affair. They spend increasing amounts of time away from the family. They may spend large quantities of money on trips and expensive presents. They will risk money, marriage, family and career in order to be with their partner of the moment.

This form of addiction has obvious similarities to romance and relationship addiction. But in this case, the addiction is not to *attraction* or to *attachment*, but simply to sex per se. The "affair addict" is trapped in his or her compulsive behavior and cannot stop, even though he or she may try. Even guilt over what the person is doing only drives him or her into sexual acting out yet again.

Affair addicts are likely convinced that what they are doing is not really wrong. They may tell themselves they simply have a stronger sex drive than other people or are somehow more sexually appealing to others than most people. They may rationalize, in the face of all reason and all evidence to the contrary, that their affairs bring new life to their marriage. In a society that largely condones extramarital adventurism, it can take a long time for an affair addict to recognize the depth of his or her problem and seek help.

However, multiple affairs do not provide enough thrills for very long. Sex addiction may escalate to perverse forms of sex involving bondage, masochism or sadism. Addicts may pursue sex with multiple partners or begin seeing prostitutes. All these derivative behaviors reflect the ever-diminishing satisfactions of addictive sex devoid of intimacy.

Level Three

Long after it has become unhealthy and immoral, sex addiction progresses to the point where it crosses the criminal line. Level three refers to relatively minor criminal behaviors, such as prostitution, which is sometimes mistakenly referred to as a "victimless" crime, and which some experts would like to see "decriminalized." Some sex addicts will spend hundreds of dollars a night on prostitutes. Believing themselves to be practicing "free love," they are actually enslaved to the world's oldest profession.

Other level three acts include voyeurism and exhibitionism. Such acts may not be as outwardly obvious as they sound. A jogger who looks in bedroom windows as he or she passes can be just as much a voyeur as the person who hides in the bushes and spies on a target. An exhibitionist might do nothing more than leave the shades open while changing clothes at home or leave his or her fly unzipped when in public.

All these acts are illegal, though they usually bear only minor consequences to their victims and minor legal sanctions for their perpetrators. More serious infractions constitute the fourth level of sex addiction.

Level Four

Child molestation, incest and rape are behaviors that characterize the fourth level of sex addiction. The perpetrator—which is what the person will now be called by the police—will do jail time if apprehended. The victim will pay an even heavier price—often a life sentence of emotional turmoil and pain. He or she may well grow up to victimize others, repeating the chain of addiction across the generations. This never-ending cycle of victimization should move all of us to confront the sex addict and help the person get the treatment he or she needs.

The Addiction Cycle

Obsession	Personal pain
	Emotional or sexual trigger
	Mind saturated with sexual thoughts
The Hunt	Search for sex "object"
	Place to masturbate
	Pornography
	Sexual partner
	Often highly ritualized
Recruitment	Purchase or proposition

Gratification	Orgasm by whatever means
	Ritualistic sex
Return to normal	Brief interlude
	Obsession lifts
Justification	"It wasn't so bad"
	"Everyone does it"
	"I needed/deserved it"
Blame	Seek scapegoat
	Anyone can be target
	Shirk personal responsibility
Shame	Guilt and remorse
	Bottom rung of society
Despair	Greater pain than before acting out
	Hopelessness
Promises	"Never again!"
	Promises trigger obsessive thinking
	Cycle starts over again

The Addiction Cycle

We can identify the same cycle as in romance addiction or relationship addiction. The stages of sex addiction progress from relatively minor to extremely severe. The consequences—for addicts, their victims and their families—likewise grow more severe. The addiction is painful for sex addicts at *any* stage.

Sex addicts are usually laboring under their own denial, so deeply trapped in the addictive cycle that they cannot see any way of escape. Understanding the stages in that cycle can make it easier for sex addicts—and for those around them—to identify the problem and choose to seek help.

Obsession

Sex addiction begins with a severe focus on self, either the "poor-me" variety or an obsession with past hurts. The addict loses the ability to concentrate on daily life as his or her mind becomes saturated with thoughts of how he or she will obtain relief.

The triggers of obsessive thinking can be anger, shame, pain, anxiety or some other momentary emotional upset. Or the trigger can be sexual in nature: some form of pornography, an attractive individual glimpsed in passing, or an innocent-looking picture in a magazine, on television or online that stirs up lust. Whatever the trigger, the addict feels compelled to find relief as soon as possible.

The Hunt

Eventually, the sex addict is driven to action. The addict looks for something or someone with which to express his or her sexual desires. The person may seek out a familiar bookstore or nightclub to obtain pornography. He or she may go out in search of a sexual partner, perhaps in a singles' bar or on the street. Or the addict may simply find a bathroom where he or she can be alone in order to fantasize and masturbate. The hunt is often highly ritualized, built on years of practiced behavior and experience.

Recruitment

Identifying and obtaining a victim may be as simple as purchasing a magazine or dropping quarters into a slot at a peep show. Or it may be far more complex, as in enticing and seducing an unsuspecting person.

Gratification

On the one hand, gratification is simply a matter of achieving orgasm, by means ranging from masturbation to intercourse. But it is not always so simple. Many sex addicts cannot achieve orgasm apart from elaborate— and ever-escalating—fantasy fulfillment. Finding the right kind of pornography, the right kind of partner or the right brand of perverse sexual behavior is what fuels the addictive process from one level to the next.

Return to Normal

After the fantasy has been fulfilled and orgasm achieved, the obsession lifts and the addict once again feels "normal." Ted Bundy even described a feeling of normalcy after committing a murder. But as with other kinds of addiction, this state of normalcy does not last. Reality intrudes, starting the cycle over again.

Justification

As the addict allows himself or herself to become aware of what he or she has done, the need arises to justify it. Addicts are accomplished mental gymnasts, going through colossal logical contortions to persuade themselves that it was really okay, no one was hurt and everyone does it.

> **Addicts are accomplished mental gymnasts, going through colossal logical contortions to persuade themselves that it was really okay, no one was hurt and everyone does it.**

Blame

When the addict can no longer believe his or her own rationalizations, the addict seeks a scapegoat onto whom he or she can project his or her problems. The addict looks for someone to blame for the dreadful feelings that always resurface when the euphoria of gratification wears off. The individual will blame his or her parents, spouse, society and even God. The addict will blame almost anyone rather than accept personal responsibility for his or her actions.

Shame

As the addict finds it increasingly difficult to project onto others what he or she has done, guilt and shame set in and eat away at the addict's soul. The individual feels bad, less for what he or she has *done* than for what he or she has *become*. The addict sees himself or herself as occupying the bottom rung of society.

Despair

Eventually, the addict reaches a point where the pain is greater *after* acting out than it was *before*. The addict feels hopeless to change. At this point, the addict may turn to drinking or may augment his or her sexual addiction with any of a dozen other compulsions, all in a desperate attempt to make the hurt go away. Suicide becomes a distinct possibility.

Promises

The addict tells himself or herself, and others, that it will never happen again. The addict will never go to "that place" again. He or she will never see "that person" again. But the addict's promises serve only to refocus his or her obsessive thinking and trigger the addictive process yet again.

Sex addicts are on a collision course with family and personal disintegration. In their wake frequently lies a trail of ruined relationships, where lust supplanted love in the drive for sexual gratification on demand. The victims feel needed—for a time. Then they simply feel used. Often it will be their response to the addict's treatment of them that helps determine whether the sex addict will awaken to his or her problem and seek help, before it is too late. (See appendix B to assess whether you may have a sexual addiction.)

Note
1. For an edited version of that interview, see James C. Dobson, *Life on the Edge* (Dallas, TX: Word Publishing, 1995), pp. 193-200.

CHAPTER 5

Origins of People Addictions

Elizabeth's father was a seething, angry man who worked as a long-distance trucker. He was a loner and had few friends. Whenever he got to know anyone, it wasn't long before he picked a fight with them and destroyed the friendship. These bursts of temper affected his family, too.

On more than one occasion, he had become so unruly that his wife had to call the police to the house. What most people would have considered child abuse was, in the mind of Elizabeth's father, nothing more than strict discipline. He had beaten her on numerous occasions. Elizabeth had learned the phrase "domestic violence" by the time she was six years old.

Needless to say, Elizabeth was terrified of her father. She dreaded the sound of his truck pulling up to the house, knowing it would not be long before either she or her mother would be the victims of an angry man who could become enraged at the slightest provocation. Affection and nurturing were out of the question.

Even in his rare, pleasant moods, the most attention Elizabeth ever got from her father was a pat on the rear or a playful punch on the arm. She longed for a *real* father, someone to hold her and tell her he loved her. Elizabeth wanted someone—*anyone*—to notice her and to pay attention to what she said and did. She wanted to make a *difference* to someone.

Her mother tried to make up for what her father failed to provide, but her mother's affection meant little to her. Elizabeth was angry at her mother, both for not making her father different and for ever having married him in the first place. She couldn't understand why her mother hadn't packed both of them up and gotten away.

Elizabeth was 10 years old when she noticed a sudden and dramatic change in her father. While he was away on a trip, a fellow trucker had persuaded him to attend an old-fashioned revival meeting in a small town in Alabama. That night revolutionized his life. In response to the evangelist's invitation, her father had come forward and committed his life to God. With that one colossal step of faith, the anger that had boiled within him for so long began to subside, replaced by a remarkable love.

When he came back from the trip, the changes he had told Elizabeth's mother about over the phone quickly became apparent. He held Elizabeth and her mother in his arms. He wept. He asked their forgiveness for the way he had treated them. He promised that from then on, things would be different.

Elizabeth was both excited and apprehensive. She could hardly believe what had happened, nor could she bring herself to believe it would last. She waited for her father to revert to his old ways. He never did. The anger and violence had simply disappeared, in a way that could only be described as miraculous.

But by the same token, her father never really became comfortable with displaying his feelings. He worked hard at being a good father and at rebuilding his marriage. But he remained distant, aloof. Happy as she was by the marvelous change in her father, Elizabeth gloomily realized that her dream of a warm, affectionate, loving father was still just that—a dream.

She began reaching out for the affection she craved from others, especially the boys she met in school. By age 15, Elizabeth was beautiful, popular and sexually very active. She dated lots of boys and slept with most of them.

Elizabeth reaped the consequences of her promiscuity. Even through three abortions and two miscarriages, she continued to search for the affection her father never gave her. She felt driven to conquer every new male she met. Sex was never the motivation. All she wanted was to be held and told she was loved. Sex was simply the price she had learned to pay for what she wanted. Elizabeth longed for intimacy and thought that by being sexual she was obtaining it.

By the time she turned 20, Elizabeth was addicted to relationships and dependent on the "love" she felt when seduction brought her close to a male.

Filling the Void

It is remarkably common at treatment centers to hear a woman patient say, "I'm sort of a sex addict—but not really. I guess I'm more of a love addict. The sex was just a necessary evil." How many women have misused sex in a vain quest for love and attention, and suffered the horrible consequences of unwanted pregnancy, abortion and sexually transmitted disease as a result? How many, in a desperate search for love and affection, have resorted to sex in order to feel something?

Like Elizabeth, many men and women have learned that no amount of romance, no relationship and no sexual encounter will ever fill the void left by years of childhood neglect and abuse. A lonely and unfulfilled childhood all too often forms the basis for a lonely and unfulfilled adulthood. With striking regularity, one of the common denominators of romance, relationship and sex addicts is the futile search for attention and affection stemming from a childhood characterized by major unmet needs.

A stream of water, rushing down hill under the force of gravity, will *always* find its way to the bottom. Once started on its course, it will relentlessly press onward. If it is blocked at one turn, it will either branch out in a new direction or else accumulate enough force to burst its temporary dam.

Addiction is much the same. Like the flowing source of a powerful stream, it will always find ways to express itself. Addiction propels obsessive thinking and compulsive behavior. If it is stopped at one turn—by changing circumstances, perhaps, or by the exercise of will power—addiction will either branch out in a new direction or build up force until it bursts free of all restraints.

That is why, ultimately, all addictions must be dealt with by going to the source. Treating one set of symptoms will only cause another set of symptoms to break out. Individuals who struggle with addictions will often go from one to another—from alcoholism to overeating, from drugs to sex—until they deal with the source of their problems. Frequently that source is found in an emotionally deprived childhood or an abusive or dysfunctional family.

How Addictions Develop

In an earlier book, *Hooked on Life*, I described at length how addictions and other compulsive behaviors develop. Since it's the key to understanding the source of romance, relationship and sex addiction, I will briefly review the main points here.

Let me begin by saying that I believe God to be the answer to all our problems. God is love, utterly other-centered. By contrast, our sinful, self-obsessed society has little ability to grasp Christ's message of self-sacrifice and service to others. It is precisely this sinful self-obsession that is the source of our problems. The lie of our culture—and the dynamic that drives addiction—is precisely the opposite: The belief that focus on the self is the answer to our problems.

Three primary areas serve as the focus of our obsession. Together they form the foundation of our personality and identity. They are the materials of which we are made, and by which we are destroyed. These three foundational areas center around the issues of identity, intimacy and adequacy.

Identity, intimacy and adequacy shape the way we deal with reality, with relationships and with responsibility. To any person with an addiction or compulsive behavior pattern, at least one of those three words—"reality," "relationships" or "responsibility"—causes a sense of unease. These areas are usually identified as personal difficulties—usually one noticeably more than the others.

Three Key Issues of Life

1. Issues of identity: Who are we?
2. Issues of intimacy: With whom are we going to be close?
3. Issues of adequacy: What are we going to do and be?

The Core Issue: Intimacy

Intimacy is usually the core issue for the romance, relationship or sex addict. It has to do with being able to give oneself to another without reservation, and with being able to receive another's gift of self with freedom and openness. Intimacy may be undermined by fear of failure in the relationship, which may be based on a long history of failures. It may be undermined by fear of rejection or of not measuring up to others' expectations—again, perhaps based on agonizing experience.

Difficulty with intimacy can spring from many sources, but the most common origin is a deprived or abused childhood. If the individual does not bring to the surface and deal with those root causes, the hope of getting free from addiction is greatly limited.

Problems with intimacy are usually coupled with self-obsession, usually in the realms of guilt, shame, fear or anger. I might feel guilty about things I have done, or about things that have been done to me. If I was molested and cannot forgive the molester, I will continue to carry a sense of guilt and shame over what happened even though I was not the one who did wrong. If I was victimized—perhaps abused in some way—and have not come to grips with what happened and why, the fear of a recurrence will cloud my relationships, making it impossible for me to freely give myself to another person.

In the absence of intimacy, addicts look for substitutes. Everything they do becomes an attempt to find relief; all other considerations become secondary.

Such fear is but a form of self-obsession. If I am focused on trusting God and serving others, I need not fear the outcome. If I can forgive those who have harmed me, I need no longer be bound by the hurt they caused me.

As I have noted earlier, addicts are very angry people. Their anger feeds on itself as they reflect endlessly on how they have been hurt and on what the world owes them. If they remain angry about something that happened 20 years ago, then everything in their lives will be tainted by anger. They cannot relate to others intimately, because their anger blocks their giving of self.

In the absence of intimacy, addicts look for substitutes. They may look to drinking, spending money, working, gambling, romance, relationships, food, sex, drugs or other things to fill the void. Everything they do becomes an attempt to find relief; all other considerations become secondary. If no single substitute suffices—and none possibly can—addicts will look to additional ones. This explains why addictions so often seem to occur in clusters. Each new compulsion represents an attempt to cover some basic need or problem that the original addiction could not resolve.

Since intimacy is the fundamental problem in romance, relationship and sex addiction, any accompanying addictions will also have some relationship to the intimacy void. Lack of intimacy becomes a reason to try harder, to compensate more and to seek new sources of relief. Let's consider some of the compulsive behavior problems that often accompany romance, relationship and sex addiction, and see how they relate to the root problem of intimacy.

The Overeater

There are many reasons, both conscious and unconscious, for out-of-control eating. Beyond the basic fact that eating is necessary for survival, it is also pleasurable. Satisfying the pangs of hunger feels good physically, but eating also feels good emotionally. It can provide a sense of relief from pain, or of reward for enduring trials. Eating can become a form of self-nurturing. A person who feels hurt or abandoned seeks comfort from the same source of nurture mothers use during infancy—food.

But overeating can go further than this. By becoming fat, the overeater insulates himself or herself from the world around. Compulsive overeating creates a plausible explanation for the rejection addicts have set themselves up to expect from others. Better to be rejected for the way they look than for who they are as a person. Thus, being fat becomes a way to avoid the risk of intimacy.

The Anorexic/Bulimic

Out of a fear of losing control, the anorexic and the bulimic seize on one area they know they can control absolutely: the intake of food. Anorexics virtually starve themselves. Bulimics, like overeaters, seek comfort in binge eating. But they then use severe dieting and exercise—or, more typically, self-induced vomiting—to ensure that the binge eating does not make them fat.

Usually, this manic quest for thinness is rationalized as essential to being attractive to others. In fact, the very obsessiveness that drives the process virtually eliminates any possibility of intimacy. This only further fuels the addiction to romance, relationships or sex.

The Chemically Dependent

There is a direct link between chemical dependency and the people addictions of romance, relationships and sex. When a love addict acts out and reaches the "despair" stage of the addiction cycle, there is an intense desire for immediate relief from the feelings of hopelessness and shame. Often that relief appears in the form of a drug—including alcohol.

Ironically, once the drugs or alcohol take effect, the resultant release from inhibitions frees the addict to engage in even more high-risk, value-contradictory behavior. The original quest for intimacy is now jet-propelled by the effects of the drug.

The Workaholic

Workaholism is a dysfunctional attempt to earn self-esteem by being productive. The workaholic may consider himself or herself unworthy of being loved or even noticed by others; therefore, the workaholic drives himself or herself to higher and higher levels of accomplishment in an attempt to prove his or her worth. In the process, of course, the workaholic eliminates any possibility of the human interaction that might lead to intimacy.

Conversely, the workaholic may fear intimacy and take refuge in work as a way of avoiding meaningful interaction with others. Or the workaholic may plunge himself or herself into excessive work in an effort to distract the mind from obsessive thinking, or from the feelings of shame that result from acting out his or her compulsions in the areas of romance, relationships and sex.

Recovery: All or Nothing

However many addictions an individual may have, he or she must recover from *all of them* in order to experience life to the full. People frequently focus their attention on the most obvious addiction, or on the one that is most socially acceptable, thinking it is the only one. But no sooner has one addiction been tackled than another rears its head. Sometimes, if the new addiction seems less objectionable (as, for example, when a recovering alcoholic becomes an overeater) the new addiction can actually be seen as a helpful substitute for the first—as if one disease could ever be an acceptable cure for another.

Other times, dealing with one addiction will cause another, more embarrassing one to surface—as when a recovering anorexic is driven to sex addiction. This is the more common experience. Even when people are aware of more than one problem, they will usually address the one with less stigmas attached, in the hope that "that will take care of everything."

Instead, denial is made worse by the mistaken belief that, having just dealt with one addictive problem, surely there could not be another. The person then has to hit bottom all over again before tackling the new problem.

It is sometimes possible, and always preferable, to let the pain (and consequent determination) of hitting bottom in one area motivate recovery in other areas as well. Otherwise, the person will continue to smoke, overeat or work compulsively—even while refraining successfully from romance, relationship or sex addiction. To be complete, recovery must cover *all* areas of addiction.

Ultimately, the romance, relationship or sex addict must come to grips with the issue of intimacy if he or she is to recover from these, and other, addictions. If "recovery" does not include coming to a point where genuine intimacy is possible, that recovery will be incomplete and short-lived. When genuine intimacy is achieved and maintained, the engine that drives the "love addictions" runs out of gas.

One of the main obstacles to achieving intimacy is the array of false concepts of intimacy presented by our culture. In the eyes of the world, intimacy equals "closeness," which almost always includes being sexually close. The more intimate two people are, the more sexual they will be; conversely, the more sexual two people are, the more intimate they are assumed to be. Closeness also involves such concepts as "transparency," the ability to share with another your deepest longings and vulnerabilities.

Genuine intimacy may involve being sexual and will certainly entail a high degree of transparency and vulnerability. But these are by-products of intimacy, not the thing itself. Much sexuality is oriented to self-gratification. Even "openness" and "vulnerability" can be forms of emotional exhibitionism that serve selfish needs rather than contribute to true intimacy.

Too Good to Be True?

Intimacy that's too good to be real ought to make you stop and take heed, especially when it happens fast. No matter how much you want to believe it can happen quickly, real intimacy takes time. Sharing yourself, as opposed to losing yourself, is a delicate procedure that evolves step by step.

Susanna Hoffman, "The Compellingly Intense (But Crazy) Man," *Cosmopolitan* (August 1988).

Authentic intimacy must build on authentic, biblical love, where the focus is taken off my desires, my needs and my hurts, and placed on the other person's desires, needs and hurts. The joy of genuine love is not receiving but giving, not being served but serving. It is utterly different from codependency, in which I serve another to gratify my own selfish motives. Authentic intimacy is serving another purely for their sake.

Some people have been so traumatized or neglected that, in addition to learning to give to others in a sacrificial way, they also need to learn to identify their own feelings and needs, express them to others and receive love as well as give it. Authentic intimacy involves a mutual giving of self in a way, and to a degree, that weaknesses can be shared without concern for the consequences. You become open about who you really are, rather than trying to present an "image" of openness. You also accept the other person for who he or she really is, not on the basis of an idealized image or for the sake of meeting your own needs. Ironically, this disinterested focus on others ends up yielding a great reward. You are able to experience appreciation, acceptance and love on the basis of reality rather than on the basis of a pretense.

Intimacy is one of the critical issues in romance, relationship and sex addiction. But it is not the only one. Addiction, in every form, is a means of survival. Alcoholism is not a slow form of suicide—at least, not as far as the alcoholic is concerned. Alcoholics think of drink as their best—perhaps their only—means of survival. Chronic overeaters are not consciously setting out to become obese and bring on cardiac trouble. They are trying to find enough relief from the pain to live through another day.

People addicts are no different. They long for someone or something to fill the void, close the gap, mend the broken heart. Their pain can be so intense, their sense of isolation so overwhelming, that they fear they are on the verge of a lifetime of insanity. In the hope of salving that pain and masking that isolation, they constantly seek out one more fling, one more attachment, one more affair. They see the fleeting relief it provides as their best hope for surviving the pain.

Hide and Seek

Sexually addicted adults are essentially children hiding out in grown-up bodies, hungrily seeking parents to love them unconditionally.

Charlotte Davis Kasl, *Women, Sex and Addiction* (New York: Ticknor and Fields, 1989), p. 113.

A little girl like Elizabeth, growing up in a dysfunctional family, may find many ways to cope with her pain. She may create an intricate fantasy world, one where only she can go, where everyone is loving and caring. A favorite doll or a pet may provide some solace. But the longer her needs go unmet, the more intense the pain will be, and the greater the need will be for new and more powerful survival techniques.

A young child has few tools to work with, often little more than the child's imagination. But as sexual development progresses, the child discovers the principles of attraction, flirtation and even seduction. The child finds he or she has new tools to work with: a developing personality, an expressive face, a maturing body. With these the child can draw others to himself or herself and elicit from them the romantic intoxication, the relational attention or the sexual gratification the child seeks.

Seeing an adult reach out to others in this quest for "love" is like watching a five-year-old child perform for adults in an effort to attract their attention. Addicts go from one person to the next, seeking the reassurance that someone has noticed them and that someone knows and cares that they exist. It is as though they are stuck in the childhood phase of development—where the only thing that counts is being the center of attention, where there is no thought or concern for the needs of others.

If they are lucky, their destructive survival techniques will bring them just enough relief from the pain, just enough maintenance of control, to enable them to see their problem and decide to change. Sometimes addicts will turn to religion. What appears to be a positive movement toward something good, however, is often just another survival technique. Even religion, even faith, can be undermined by unresolved issues from the past. Until those issues are faced squarely—as they can be—addicts will remain trapped in the prison of addiction.

Male and Female Differences

There appear to be some characteristic differences between males and females when it comes to romance, relationship and sex addiction. Sex addiction is far more common among men, while romance and relationship addiction is more common among women. This seems to be because the sexes approach life from opposite directions.

Women typically need attraction and attachment before they are prepared to open up sexually. Men typically seek out sexual expression before they open themselves up emotionally. Understanding the female's different orientation, the male will frequently fake being caring during the seduction process and hide behind a facade. The counterpart to this, of course, is the woman who fakes sexual pleasure "in payment" for the romance and the relational security that sex seems to offer.

Male-Female Distinctions		
	Male	*Female*
Primary type of addiction	Sex	Romance or relationship
Primary needs	Space	Security
Fears	Bound or smothered	Abandonment
Manipulations	Demands sex	Withholds sex

There are other differences as well. Fear plays an important role in all the people addictions. In men, the greatest fear is typically of being bound or smothered. In women, by contrast, the greatest fear is of being abandoned. Both fears, however, lead to the same result: avoidance of intimacy. The male avoids intimacy in order to keep from being "trapped." The female avoids it so as to lessen the chances for eventual abandonment.

Both sexes practice fundamentally dishonest and manipulative behavior. A female romance addict will withhold sex, while a male sex addict will demand it. Women frequently are looking for romance or relationship, and are willing to use sex to get it. Men are more typically looking for sex, and will feign romantic interest and commitment to get it. These characteristic behaviors seem to reinforce what are sometimes considered stereotypical gender roles. This does not, however, negate the fact that they are empirically, clinically observable.

Family Ties

I noted earlier how common it was for romance, relationship and sex addicts to have childhood abandonment or abuse, or a dysfunctional family in their background. None of us, of course, comes from a perfect family. There is no such thing. We are all products of our own particular families, each with all its weaknesses and faults.

By God's grace, we can rise above these limitations and wounds. But we will never totally escape them. The Bible talks about the sins of the fathers being visited upon subsequent generations (see Exod. 20:5). We often see this dynamic reflected in our work with addicted people.

Still, even with all its faults, with all its potential for damaging effects, the family remains God's chosen instrument for the continuation of human life and for the early development of our personalities. For us to experience a certain amount of "bad fruit" from our families even seems to be part of God's perfect plan for each of our lives. These difficulties force each of us to turn to Him to transcend problems we cannot evade.

There is a certain danger in examining the role that a dysfunctional family background can play in the development of later problems. It has become rather faddish these days to seek the source of every problem in our families—to blame our parents for everything that is wrong with us. This kind of blame shifting only makes our problems worse.

The message of recovery is always that, as free individuals casting our wills upon God, we can become responsible for our own actions. We can learn to respond redemptively to what has happened to us, rather than simply shuffle our feet and mutter: "I can't help it. It's the way I was raised. It's all my parents' fault. There's nothing I can do about it." Such an attitude undermines recovery.

Even so, it does help if we can understand the role that family dynamics play in the development of problems. If we see ourselves reflected in these principles, our response should not be to capitulate to self-pity, but to learn more dearly how we can seek God for the precise help we need to recover. Understanding the role of childhood deprivation and parental mistakes should not *excuse* us from taking personal responsibility for our lives, but should *equip* us to do it better.

With this in mind, let's look more closely at some of the early childhood dynamics that can contribute to romance, relationship and sex addiction later in life.

Victimization

Addicted adults typically were victims of a variety of abuse as children. Often their parents were so unstable and so unreliable that the individual's life becomes one long search for someone who can be counted on. In many cases, this search evolves into a series of efforts to capture and control other people. The victim then becomes a victimizer. He or she unknowingly resurrects the experiences of childhood, but in reverse fashion, this time playing the other role.

Not infrequently the addict can point to one parent or the other as the primary source of the victimization. Often an addict will organize his or her life around a resolve to be different from that parent. Ironically, this very focus on being unlike the problematic parent is in itself a way of obsessing about that parent—in particular, about that parent's very weaknesses and limitations.

Thus, perversely, the very problems the addict is trying so hard to avoid become that much more thoroughly ingrained in his or her subconscious, and eventually express themselves in his or her behavior. Again, the victim becomes the victimizer. The only way out of this vicious cycle is for addicts to learn how not to establish their identity in reference to other people—how to break out of the trap of seeing themselves, fundamentally, as victims.

Unhealthy Parents, Unhealthy Children

Parents of addicted adults are not always blatant victimizers, in the sense of being sexually or physically abusive. There are other, more subtle ways in which nurturing is withheld and the child's development is undermined. Parents caught up in their own pursuits and problems either fail to notice their children's needs or simply don't care about them.

Many addicts look back on their early family life and see the results of such factors as divorce or marital strife, workaholism, subsequent absenteeism by one or both parents, or even such addictive problems as alcoholism or drug abuse. Children are often blind to the signs and symptoms of such problems while they are growing up, but are able to discern it easily when—as adults who have been educated on the topic—they look back over their early lives. Then they also are able to see in themselves the signs and symptoms of codependency, and understand themselves as, for example, "adult children of alcoholics."

Addicted, codependent or otherwise troubled parents frequently develop unhealthy patterns of coping with reality, which they pass on to their children. Sensing control of their own lives slipping away, they attempt to control everything around them. They develop a rigid structure of expectations, which is impossible for the child to meet. Then, when the child falls short, there is intense criticism and ridicule.

The parents may hold children to a hidden set of rules of which even they are only dimly conscious. Everyone walks on eggshells, trying to avoid breaking a rule that no one even acknowledges exists. Such an environment can be extremely damaging. The rigid "my way or no way at all" atmosphere constrains the child's development, simultaneously binding him or her to the parent even as the urge to separate grows stronger.

This area is one of the clearest examples of the "sin of the fathers" being carried from one generation to the next (see Exod. 20:5). It is likely that the addict's rigid or abusive parents learned their dysfunctional approaches from their parents, and so on up the line. The precise form of the problem might change: Sexual abuse in one generation might be replaced by workaholism in the next; alcoholism in one generation might give rise to relationship addiction in the next.

The degree and intensity of the problem will also vary from generation to generation, depending on how various individuals take personal responsibility for their choices and responses to what has happened to them. Until recovery is initiated and a clean break is made from seeing oneself, and responding to life's problems, as a victim, the legacy of dysfunction is apt to continue.

Parental Death and Illness

Another common experience of romance, relationship and sex addicts is the death or chronic illness of a parent. This is another circumstance that often gives rise to a dysfunctional or inadequate family life, one which seems especially cruel because the cause of the dysfunction is "nobody's fault."

When an addict can point back to a parent's alcoholism or physical abusiveness, there is at least some culpability to be assigned. But when a parent dies or is taken ill, dealing with the resultant dislocations is made even more painful by the fact that there is no one to blame.

> # Bob shunned intimacy in order to make sure he was never trapped in a relationship that might suddenly end on him. He made sure that he would be the one who did the abandoning.

Illness or death will sometimes cause a family to rally together, strengthening its character and deepening its roots. But many families do not have the proper foundation to grow from adversity.

Bob was a recovering cocaine addict and unmarried sex addict. He remembers the time he was telling his mother about his day at school when she suddenly clutched her heart and collapsed onto the kitchen floor. She died instantly. Bob was 11 years old.

The sudden and traumatic disappearance of his mother produced in him a grave fear of abandonment. In his case, he shunned intimacy in order to make sure he was never trapped in a relationship that might suddenly end on him. He made sure that he would be the one who did the abandoning. It wasn't until age 35 that he began to recover from his cocaine addiction, which brought his sex addiction to light and, in turn, enabled him to see for the first time the intimacy issue that lay hidden beneath his other problems.

Linda's mother was ill throughout most of her teenage years. Bedridden with a lung disorder, she had little time and less energy to devote to Linda. Other family members had little involvement in her life as well. Their attention had to be devoted to caring for Mom. One day, an ambulance arrived and carried Linda's mother away. She never returned.

Linda felt devastated. Now there was no hope of ever having the kind of relationship with her mother that she heard her friends talk about. And she hadn't even had a chance to say goodbye! Her father remarried quickly in an attempt to "put the past behind him." His focus on his new wife only left Linda feeling more alone and abandoned than ever.

By the time Linda left high school, she was seeking the attention and affection she needed from men. She was 28 when she finally sought treatment for relationship addiction.

The Family's View of Sex

All of us derive our basic orientation toward sex from our parents and the way they raise us. Romance, relationship and sex addicts seem typically to have one of two extreme views. The first is a promiscuous, even seductive view. This often occurs in cases where the individual has been sexually abused.

Parents may not cross the incest line, but nevertheless do things that are destructive. They may make suggestive statements about the way a son or daughter dresses. Their embraces may be more than merely affectionate. Such behaviors can accelerate the child's sexual awakening and impulses, and can be very confusing and frustrating. Children fail to develop intimacy skills since they have instead learned to relate to others in sexual ways.

The other extreme view of sex is severely inhibited. It often stems from the belief on the part of the parents that sex is "evil" or "dirty." Even the slightest passing reference to the subject brings glares of disapproval; frank and open discussion is out of the question. Children raised in such an environment often fear anything sexual. They dress so as to make themselves unappealing to others. Any thoughts of a sexual nature produce guilt and shame.

At the same time, these children's enforced ignorance and fear of sex can make it seem that much more attractive: the classic forbidden fruit syndrome. This powerful desire for something they believe to be seriously wrong can set the stage for serious personality tensions.

One girl, for example, rigidly suppressed any and all sexual feelings for years. Then, while she was in high school, the dam burst and she went through a succession of relationships with boys. She would allow them to take liberties with her up to the point of intercourse; then, she would suddenly end the relationship and move on to someone else. She grew into adulthood utterly confused about her sexuality and well on her way to a powerful romance addiction.

When parents either fail to teach their children about sexuality, or when they teach them a distorted view, it causes imbalance in the child's perception of self and of the opposite sex. Both extremes—permissive and repressive—short-circuit the development of intimacy skills and help set the stage for romance, relationship and sex addiction in later life.

Male and Female Role Models

Boys and girls need fathers and mothers. That is, children of both sexes need role models of both sexes. In the normal family, parents provide this role modeling, both of whom are fully accessible to children of either sex. When this is not the case, imbalance and disorder can result.

For example, a man who was not nurtured by his mother may seek to conquer females sexually as a twisted substitute for that missing maternal attention. This same dynamic may take the form of using pornography or engaging the services of prostitutes.

Conversely, a boy engulfed by an overbearing and overprotective mother will be unable to develop his own identity in a healthy way. The "mama's boy" may appear to enjoy the doting attention, but he eventually grows to resent the trap he cannot spring. As an adult, he aims to avoid ever being "smothered" again by seeking to control women, eliminating any possibility of vulnerability and intimacy. He moves from woman to woman, always trying to establish dominance over a mother figure.

The combination of an overbearing mother and an absent or distant father—a common combination in our society—can compound the problem in various ways. The smothering mom, feeling abandoned by her husband, clings all the more resolutely to her son, believing he is "all she has in life." When the father is present, he is apt to be abrasive and even violent, causing the mother to envelop her son even more tightly.

The boy in such a family is likely to grow up with a welter of confused feelings toward his parents. He wants to be freed from his mother, whose domination he resents. But he holds his father guiltless, not realizing that it is the father's abandonment of the mother that contributes to her insecurity and manipulativeness. Such a boy may grow up to exhibit extraordinarily harsh attitudes toward women. Or he may turn to homosexuality in an effort to find male affection and avoid female control.

A girl raised in the same dominant-mother, absent-father environment will frequently seek to escape from her mother and then seek out men to replace the missing father influence. Not knowing how to relate to men, she may utilize sex as her only means of cementing a connection with a male.

Conversely, a girl raised without an adequate female role model may grow up insecure about her identity as a woman, unable to feel "okay" about herself except in terms of her relationship to a man. Such a woman, with her need for the security of attachment, can become a prime candidate for relationship addiction.

Three Key Family Traits

Romance, relationship and sex addiction typically build on three traits common to dysfunctional families. These traits characterize the family environment and are passed on from parent to child. They are traits that help create a climate in which addiction can flourish.

Poor Communication

One of the most common features of dysfunctional families is that they have secrets they want to keep hidden, painful realities they want to deny—Dad's drunkenness, Mom's obesity and so on.

When children begin to be aware of these things, their impulse is to acknowledge them as the obvious realities they are, ask questions and try to change them. But all such attempts are met with unmistakable signals that the topic is off-limits. These questions are rebuffed by angry responses, even punishment.

Or the child may simply note that none of the adults around him or her seem to acknowledge the reality of what he or she thinks is happening. Therefore, the child concludes he or she must be mistaken. Either way, the message is clear: What appears to be reality, isn't, and certain realities are to be denied. The child either adopts the adult posture of denial, thereby losing touch with reality, or clings to an awareness of what is real, thereby learning to suffer in silence.

> **Dysfunctional families have secrets they want to keep hidden, painful realities they want to deny.**

Lack of Awareness or Feelings

A child growing up in a dysfunctional family soon learns that one way to avoid being penalized for expressing how he or she feels is simply to stop feeling. Of course, it is impossible to simply shut off the emotions. What really happens is that feelings are repressed or denied. They still hurt, but the child pretends they do not.

Adults with this kind of background are often emotionally numb. They are unable to identify their emotions, to describe how they feel. Thus, they are unable to deal with them constructively. Their feelings "just happen," impacting them in ways they cannot influence or prevent. This generates tremendous pressure to find some source of relief from the pain, some way to control their seemingly inexplicable and uncontrollable inner state. Some sort of addiction often appears as the answer.

Fantasy is a frequent tool that children employ to escape the reality of their feelings. They invent imaginary worlds where everything is fine and everyone is happy, where the problems destroying the family do not exist. This early use of fantasy as a vehicle of escape obviously lends itself to both romance and sex addiction in later life.

Lack of Trust

Children in dysfunctional families learn not to trust others. Their experience tells them that other people either don't mean what they say or are incapable of following through on what they promise. What other lesson can be drawn from a father whose workaholism always gets in the way of the little league games he has promised to attend? Or a mother whose alcoholism means she constantly forgets to pick you up after school or is physically unable to do so?

Obviously, children lose their trust in parents who are abusive toward them, whether verbally, physically or sexually. They are placed in the double bind of knowing that "what Dad is doing to me is wrong," and at the same time trying to believe that "Dad loves me." It is like being slapped and kissed at the same time.

When the other parent either ignores the problem or insists it does not exist, trust is eroded still further. And, of course, when one parent becomes absent (whether through death, divorce or plain desertion), the resulting sense of abandonment destroys trust altogether. Whatever the cause, growing up unable to trust others—suspecting everyone around you plans to abuse, betray or abandon you—leads to extreme control needs and severe aversion to vulnerability. (See appendix C to help you determine the roots of your addiction.)

The Way Out

Children from a sick home have a weak foundation on which to build their lives. It is as though they hit a roadblock in their development and never move beyond it. They arrive at adulthood with an immature and irresponsible character that sets them up for difficult relationships. They see others through the lens of their own pain and distorted self-image. They feel ashamed about their past and about the unhealthy behaviors they are presently using to cope with it. Life is burdensome, difficult. They feel they are all alone in facing their problems.

In a desperate effort to escape the pain, such people often run from God, too. Overwhelmed by trying to make it on their own, they resist allowing a higher power to help them. Childhood lessons about God are dismissed along with everything else as unreliable and possibly dangerous. The harder life becomes, the more resentful they grow toward a God who, it seems clear, "has it in for them." Their belief that God is angry at them increases their anger at the rest of the world.

Whether it is the intoxication of romance, dependency on relationships or the compulsion to have sex, people who are "addicted to love" have certain common denominators. Prominent among these is invariably a childhood marked by abuse, neglect, abandonment and unhealthy role models.

The only way out for those people who grew up in a dysfunctional family is to learn to take personal responsibility for who they are and what they will become. True, they experienced great trauma early on, but the "poor me, blame everyone" response must stop. True, they were victims in the objective sense of the word, but they must now learn to reject self-identification as a "victim"—to stop seeing themselves that way and to stop relating to others in that role. They can choose to stop playing the victim. If they do not, the result will only be continued misery and victimization of others.

The process of recovery is different for romance, relationship and sex addicts, not only because the three addictions are different, but also because each individual is unique. Still, as there are common denominators among the problems, there are also common denominators among the recovery processes.

People who suffer from these addictions must reach a determination to uncover the source of their problem and deal with it. They must resolve to live life as a mature adult, taking appropriate responsibility for their choices and the consequences of those choices. Ultimately, they

need to replace their unhealthy dependency on other people with surrender to the will of God.

CHAPTER 6

What Keeps the Addict Addicted?

The rumors ran rampant.

John Jacobs was the head of a large, well-known Christian ministry. Rumors were constantly swirling about his flings with women other than his wife. There were even reports that he had moved some of his female employees to headquarters so he could have easier access to them—as though he were living out some Old Testament fantasy of having a harem, like King David.

Many people in the organization knew of the problem and were distressed by it. But they did nothing about it. *He's been getting away with it for years,* some told themselves. *Why should I be the one to bring down this ministry? Besides, what will happen to all these employees—what will happen to me—if word of this leaks out?*

John's wife also knew of his affairs. Once she had even found John in a hotel room with a woman from their church. She was hurt and depressed, but she did nothing. She felt it was her duty to stand by her man. She didn't want to be the one responsible for destroying his ministry, either. John explained to her that his needs were simply greater than those of other men, that he had no choice but to satisfy them. She didn't really buy that, but she rationalized that unless she accepted it and looked the other way, her marriage would be destroyed.

In time, John's problem grew worse. He did outrageous things, things that almost seemed like attempts to get caught. He visited bars that featured nude dancing. He would call "dial-a-stripper" to his hotel room when attending Christian conferences away from home. Once he was even arrested for soliciting a prostitute that turned out to be an undercover police officer. When the police found out who he was, they sheepishly gave him a warning and let him go. They didn't want to risk the bad publicity that would come from arresting a prominent minister on a morals charge. It appeared that John could do whatever he chose and get away with it.

It appeared that way, at least, until a lawsuit was filed against him by one of his former lovers. She claimed she had come to John's organization for help. When John saw her in the hallway, he invited her to his office for a "private consultation." He told her that ordinarily he didn't get involved in these kinds of matters, but that in her case he would make an exception.

The young lady was flattered by the offer of personal counseling from the famous minister. A week later, she was in bed with him. Her lawsuit claimed that John had later terminated the relationship, leaving her emotionally devastated and in worse condition than when she had come in for counseling.

It wasn't the first time a woman had threatened legal action. In past instances, a little private persuasion from John's lawyer—and, often, a little money under the table from the ministry's coffers—had taken care of things. But not this time. This time the woman went public, and John's house of cards came crashing down. He was forced to step down from his position as head of the organization.

While his ministry ended, his problem did not. John claimed it was all behind him now. He had been cleansed and forgiven, he said. He had been healed. But in reality, he had not been healed. His lust flared up in the presence of attractive women just as much as it ever had. And while he had lost his position, he had lost none of his smooth charm. The womanizing continued.

John's wife knew nothing had really changed. But she still refused to leave him or even to threaten leaving. She remained faithful to her marriage vow as she waited for God to change her husband. Some months later, John moved out of his home and moved in with one of his new companions. He stayed with her awhile, then grew tired of her and moved in with another woman. Still, his wife did not divorce him. She believed that one day he would come to his senses and come home to her.

He never did. Three years after leaving his wife, John filed for a divorce, which was granted speedily under the state's "no-fault" divorce law. He moved to California and became a radio talk show host. To this day, so far as I know, he has never sought help for his problem. I doubt he even thinks he has a problem.

John's story illustrates how long an addict can live out his or her problem, with the full awareness of those around him or her, without anyone taking steps to intervene. His case is particularly tragic because of all the harm it caused. Many people were thrown out of work when John's ministry collapsed. Many more were disillusioned to learn that a man of his prominence and apparent anointing could be involved in such blatant sin. The cause and reputation of Christ were dragged through the mud.

John's employees, his followers and his wife—to say nothing of his string of female victims—could all have been spared unnecessary grief if *someone* had *somehow* stepped in and insisted that John change and seek help. His board of directors could have done this. His wife could have done it. Any of the earlier women whom John seduced could have done it. But none of them did. And all of them paid the price, along with John.

Addiction: A View from the Inside

What is it like to be addicted to love? I once posed this question to a young man who had come to a treatment center. He answered bluntly,

"It's miserable. People probably imagine the joys of sex, of an unending orgy. They don't know about the other side. It hurts. I feel so guilty. The worst part is, I don't think anyone cares whether I live or die."

By the time this young man's treatment was completed, his attitudes about himself and his life had changed. But his comments are a remarkably precise summary of how men and women caught in the grip of people addictions feel about themselves and others. The life of someone addicted to love is far different from what most people imagine.

In working with romance, relationship and sex addicts, I have met some truly wonderful people. They are not "bad" people. They are just very wounded people, who have used some very counterproductive methods to cope with their pain. While others were laying a solid foundation on which to build a productive life, these people had to spend their days frantically trying to fill in the cracks of a broken foundation. But the mortar they used washed away as quickly as they tried to fill each new crevice.

Let's take a closer look at some of the dynamics that characterize the life of someone addicted to love—the things that keep the addict addicted.

Benefits of Addiction

It may seem absurd to speak of addiction as having benefits, but the addict, through his or her skewed perspective, does perceive this lifestyle as having attractive features. For one thing, it provides relief, or at least diversion, from pain. It offers temporary escape from the struggle with reality.

Addiction offers a sense of security. Obsessive thinking enables the addict to dwell in an emotional environment that is predictable and familiar. Romance addicts feel comfortable within the realm of their fantasies. Relationship addicts feel secure in their attachment to another person. Sex addicts feel powerful and "in control" as they act out their sexual drives.

Instant gratification is one benefit that romance, relationship and sex addiction all have in common. The whole point of addictive behavior is that it works right now. There is no lengthy, laborious process of developing genuine intimacy or authentic commitment. There is no need for deferred gratification. Addiction provides a quick fix to all life's problems—or so it seems.

Addiction provides a quick fix to all life's problems—or so it seems.

Quest for Security

It is not hard to see why a person might choose to hang onto a lifestyle that offers perceived benefits—even if all these "benefits" later prove to be problems in their own right. But there are other, less benign, factors in the question of why addicts stay addicted.

The lack of childhood nurturing, so common among people addicts, causes a high degree of fear and anxiety. Consequently, the addict's life is marked by a never-ending search for safety and security. Obsession over their own pain makes it impossible for addicts to genuinely love another person.

Love requires giving, and addicts feel they have nothing to give. It is all taking, in the desperate drive to soothe an aching soul. Each new romantic interlude brings a fleeting sense of safety. Each new relationship holds out the promise of emotional security. Each new sexual encounter drives away the gnawing anxiety and loneliness, if only for a moment.

But no one can make up for a lifetime of pain in one episode of ersatz—imitation—love. As soon as the intoxication of romance fades, as soon as the new relationship fizzles, as soon as the passion of sex subsides, reality comes crashing in again. The fear of being abandoned returns. The addict resumes his or her quest for that evanescent sensation of security and inner peace.

This desire for safety and security is the biggest barrier standing between the addict and an intimate relationship. Fear prevents the addict from "letting go" and making himself or herself vulnerable with another person. And without vulnerability, there is no possibility of intimacy. An addict's relationships are all take and no give. The benefits from them are hollow, superficial and short-lived. Whatever pleasure they bring masks the fear only for a moment. Fear soon returns, along with guilt and the frustration of seeing yet another attempt at self-healing go up in flames.

However grown-up the addict may seem to be on the outside, on the inside a child whimpers for attention, pleading for a mother or father to hold and reassure him or her "everything's okay, you're safe now."

A Facade of Strength

Those addicted to romance, relationships and sex are great compensators. They disguise what is lacking on the inside with an outer facade of strength. Facades take many forms: possessions, accomplishments, good looks, stylish clothes, fame, hard work, good deeds. Any and all of these can be used to build an outer wall of respectability. Until addicts find God, the creator of all value, and allow Him to give them a proper sense of self-worth, they will continue in search of more building blocks from which to erect their facade.

Intensity Instead of Intimacy

What people addicts lack in intimacy, they frequently try to make up for in intensity. They are often very tightly wound. Some persuade themselves that their very intensity of focus is intimacy. Others use their intensity as a shield against intimacy.

Either way, their intensity makes them like marathon runners who start the race too quickly. Addicts use all their energy in one burst at the beginning of the race and have nothing left by the midway point. Eventually, addicts, like the runners, "hit the wall." The pain overwhelms their depleted capacity to endure, and they simply collapse.

After a while, addicts get up, get back on the track and make the same mistake all over. They burst into a sprint once again, this time running out of steam even earlier than before, collapsing in even greater agony than before. Being unequipped to cultivate genuine intimacy, addicts settle for a manufactured substitute that seems to do the trick—at least for a while.

Pain: Hidden and Not-So-Hidden

The life of the man or woman addicted to love is, as I have noted repeatedly, a life of seeking relief from pain. Dr. Lawrence J. Hatterer, professor of psychology at Cornell University Medical School, and a man with 30 years experience in the field of addiction, summarizes the process this way:

> Addicts don't use sex for affection or recreation, but for the management of pain or anxiety.[1]

Addicts seek healing. But in the seeking, they impale themselves again and again on false solutions that only make matters worse. What could hurt more than to try to heal yourself, and in the process, cause yourself even greater misery?

People respond to pain in a variety of ways. Some try to bury it, but pain is always buried alive. It grows in silence until it demands to be felt. Physical illness, psychological disorders and emotional stress can all result from repressed pain.

Other people try to run from pain. They fill their schedules and redouble their pace, trying to distract themselves from their agony. They seem to think that if they could just go fast enough, they could outrun their feelings. But pain is patient; it always catches up.

All such efforts are ultimately doomed. Until addicts make a decision to confront their pain head-on in recovery, it will hound them without mercy.

Fear of Abandonment

Most people addicts have experienced abandonment in one form or another—ranging from severe emotional isolation to actual desertion by one or both parents—at some point in their lives. A typical form of early abandonment is the divorce of the addict's parents. A child of divorce quickly formulates the realization that if Mom and Dad can abandon each other, they can certainly abandon him or her as well. Fearing this, the child might cling even to an abusive parent, perhaps calculating that this parent has the greatest need for companionship and thus will be the least likely to discard the child.

This sets a pattern of clinging to abusive partners, based on the unwitting belief that abusiveness is a sign of need, making a long-term relationship more of a possibility. This unhealthy kind of relationship is actually viewed as safe by someone to whom even physical violence is preferable to the fear of being abandoned.

Fear of abandonment is also a reason why people addicts will seek out multiple partners. It is a way of hedging your bets: If you are hanging onto a number of people, you lessen the potential for devastation should one of those people depart.

Victimization

Those addicted to love are victimizers. Having been victims themselves for most of their lives, and knowing how controlled they felt in that role, they victimize others in an effort to gain control.

Moreover, having been in the victim role most of their lives, it is the only basis on which they know how to relate to others. Victims can identify and empathize only with other victims. Thus, one way to establish common ground with another person is to force that person into the role of victim.

It would seem that the last thing addicts would want to do is to put someone else through the same torture they themselves have endured. But that is not the motivation. Addicts are simply looking for someone who can understand their torment—even if they have to inflict that torment on someone else in order to bring it about.

Confusion About Needs

There is a difference between a need and a want. Romance, relationship and sex addicts are largely incapable of drawing the distinction. Many of their behaviors are driven by desires—very strong desires, to be sure—and not by needs. The addict justifies them by rationalizing that they stem from irresistible basic needs. Addicts believe that their needs are different from other people's needs. They believe they have unique needs that others do not share and cannot understand.

> # Sex addicts rank their need for sex on the same plane as their need for food and water. Without sex, they do not believe they can survive.

Romance addicts come to believe, for example, that intoxicating romantic encounters are fundamental needs for them. Relationship addicts think the same thing about their attachments. Sex addicts become convinced that their sexual needs are simply much stronger than other people's needs. They rank their need for sex on the same plane as their need for food and water. Without sex, they do not believe they can survive. They reject the comparison that others can live a normal life without gratifying sexual drives in the same ways, and to the same extent, that they themselves do. "But I've got to have it" is a common slogan among the sexually addicted.

In a healthy relationship, attraction, attachment and sex all play a helpful role. Romantic attraction initializes the relationship. Attachment and commitment stabilize it. Sex consummates and cements it. All work together to form a complete union of persons, which is the ultimate objective.

Not so for someone addicted to love. For those people, one or more of the three components grows all out of proportion to the others and becomes the ultimate objective in its own right. In the addict's mind, this is merely a reflection of the fact that that component is a fundamental need that he or she dare not—and cannot—ignore.

The addict's confusion about needs can become extraordinarily complex. The addict feels the need for security and will do anything to feel secure. But instead of doing things that might actually produce security, the addict instead goes after a quick sensation of arousal. The mood change results in a momentary sense of apparent security. The result is confusion between the sex drive and the security need. Pursuing one, the addict comes to believe that he or she needs the other.

Or the addict may feel the normal human need to belong. The addict wants to feel connected to others. Out of that desire for a sense of belonging, the addict uses romance or sex to attach to another. But the attachment is by nature fleeting. It actually prevents the addict from really belonging to someone in any significant sense.

In fact, since belonging presupposes intimacy—which frightens the addict—as intimacy approaches, the addict will actually run away and seek another person with whom to satisfy the urge for attachment. Thus a legitimate need is twisted and turned into an unhealthy, but insatiable, desire—which the addict then labels a basic need.

Double Mind, Double Life

Recovering addicts of all kinds regularly talk as if there were two people inhabiting their body. They will refer to themselves as "I" or "me" when speaking of the normal, healthy component of their personality. They will speak of "the addict in me" or "my addict" when referring to the other persona struggling to gain the upper hand in their lives.

For example, a sex addict might share with his or her recovery group, "I was walking to work when I passed a newsstand. My addict was screaming at me to stop and look at the skin magazines. But I decided not to stop."

In recovery, this duality is easy to discern, but the nonrecovering addict does not see it clearly. That does not mean, however, that he or she does not experience its effects. The addict is a double-minded person, tossed back and forth as if on the waves of the sea (see Jas. 1:5-8).

Every circumstance of life presents the addict with a confusing, even agonizing, dilemma as two "selves" fight for the upper hand.

A double mind produces a double life. As addiction grows, many of the shame-provoking behaviors associated with it begin to develop into a secondary lifestyle—a secret life of intrigue, delusion and deception. As addiction grows, its very shamefulness motivates the addict to erect a glowing "public life" as a facade.

The feelings of worthlessness generated by one life demand the manufacturing of a compensatory sense of worth in the other—not unlike the corporate embezzler who gives huge sums to charity. Thus, sex addicts may well be the most visible and active members of the Church, trying to convince themselves and others that they are not really as bad as they secretly know themselves to be.

Maintaining a double mind and a double life isn't easy. Small wonder that most addicts who seek treatment talk about how they "couldn't take the craziness any longer."

Other Addictions

Rarely will romance, relationship or sex addiction exist without at least one other addictive problem being present. Usually, the recovering addict will treat every other problem before getting around to dealing with his or her people addiction.

For many years, I worked largely with alcoholics and drug addicts, and it was very common to have to confront one of them with the obvious reality of a "love addiction." The evidence could often be seen right in the treatment center in the form of quick-forming relationships, romantic involvements and sexual encounters among the patients. From its very first edition, *Alcoholics Anonymous*, the groundbreaking textbook of the Alcoholics Anonymous (A.A.) movement, devotes an entire chapter to sex and relationship problems, reflecting the close link between the two addictions.

Other common associations can also be observed. Romance addiction is frequently accompanied by one of the various eating disorders. It is as though those who chase after the intoxication of romance build a

wall of fat around themselves as a subconscious way of warding off intimate relationships. Then they may get their romantic "fix" through novels, movies and soap operas. At the opposite extreme are anorexics who
maintain a frightful form of control over their weight while relinquish-
ing control over other parts of their lives.

In addition to alcohol, drugs and eating disorders, other common
compulsive behaviors that may accompany people addictions are gambling, spending money and stealing. It appears that the guilt, shame and
despair resulting from people addictions are so intense that other compulsive behaviors are adopted as coping mechanisms. Each addiction
stimulates and reinforces the others, and they all progress simultaneously until treatment is sought.

Since romance, relationship and sex addiction are so hard for most
people to acknowledge, seeking help for some other problem is often as
close as the people addict will get to receiving treatment for his or her
condition. Counselors in all fields of addictive and compulsive behavior
are learning to be alert to people addiction as the possible underlying
foundation of other problems.

The simultaneous development of several problems can be partly
attributed to the enormous appetites for attraction, attachment or sex
that people addicts either possess or develop. This insatiable appetite is
likely born out of despair. The addict desires to be filled, to be satisfied.
Since no experience ever produces the desired result, the addict searches
for more and more experiences to fill in the gaps.

No amount of romantic involvement, no multiplication of relationships, no amount of sex is ever enough. Indeed, each attempt at quench-
ing the fire only makes it burn hotter. Thus, the appetite literally feeds
on itself, producing ever more hopelessness, shame and guilt. Small
wonder that out-of-control people addicts begin seeking consolation
from pills, booze or other compulsive behaviors.

The Element of Risk

This spiraling cycle of addiction helps explain what nonaddicts often
find to be one of the most incomprehensible aspects of addiction: the

extraordinary high-risk behaviors in which addicts engage.

Part of the dynamic of addiction is to *increase* risk, to explore the outer edges of the forbidden. The reason has to do with the insatiable appetite that addiction produces, along with the excitement factor that often accompanies addictive behavior. Addicts regularly report that acting out gives them a rush of excitement. It makes them "feel more alive." It is almost as though they are addicted to the adrenaline rush that accompanies the addictive behavior.

Typical High-Risk Behaviors of Sex Addicts

- Having sex with your best friend's wife
- Having sex with a relative
- Having sex with a complete stranger, under circumstances that could lead to disease or even death
- Having sex in public places, where being caught is a definite possibility
- Breaking into a home and exposing oneself to a victim, or exposing oneself from a vehicle that can be easily traced
- Going into an adult bookstore or so-called massage parlor in an area where there is a high probability of being seen and recognized

---

However, as with other aspects of addiction, there is an escalation dynamic involved. That is, it takes more and more of the same stimulus to produce the same response. In the case of the excitement factor, it takes increasingly risky behavior to generate the rush of adrenaline. In time, what should be a *deterrent* to dangerous activity actually becomes an *enticement*. The drive to elevate the level of risk plays a key role in the addictive process.

Nowhere is this more clear than in regard to AIDS. By now most people are well aware of this deadly disease and that having unsafe sex— that is, sex with strangers unprotected by the use of a condom—is an open invitation to the AIDS virus. Yet, we regularly talk to recovering sex addicts for whom the threat of AIDS *increased* the desire for unsafe sex, rather than making them more cautious.

This process was largely unconscious, of course. These people were not saying to themselves, *I think I'll go out and try to contract a disease that will kill me.* Rather, it was the intense sensation of risk that drove them into ever more dangerous sexual behavior, heedless of the consequences.

A less lethal, but nevertheless quite common, variation on this theme is the woman who regularly risks becoming pregnant. One woman who came to us for help was a classic example of this high-risk behavior. She was a relationship addict who attempted to seal an attachment with a man by having sex with him. It didn't work, of course; the men would take advantage of the easy sex and then move on.

Still, this woman continued to have sex with virtually every man she dated, and she refused to use any form of birth control. Her reasoning was "good girls don't use birth control." She preferred to believe that her frequent sexual encounters "just happened." To use birth control would be to admit that they were premeditated. In recovery, she came to understand the illogic of this attitude and to see that her refusal to use birth control was actually a way of enhancing the risk of her sexual behavior.

The examples I have given—a man who deliberately risks contracting AIDS or a woman who deliberately runs the risk of getting pregnant—are obvious, even blatant ones. But all of us are familiar with more subtle examples: politicians who risk promising careers to carry on affairs in public or televangelists who cruise motels consorting with prostitutes. Is there not an element of deliberate risk enhancement in such otherwise incomprehensible behavior?

Risk Enhancers

Fear of   getting caught
getting mugged
getting hurt
contracting sexually transmitted disease
playing "AIDS roulette"
getting pregnant
being arrested and incarcerated
being publicly embarrassed

Staying Addicted

Few people understand the raw power addiction possesses. It is all-consuming. Left to run its course, addiction can lead to insanity or even death. No one knows more dearly than recovering addicts how serious the consequences of hiding from the problem can be, and no one is more frustrated than recovering addicts when another addict will not acknowledge his or her problem and take steps to get free.

Addiction is so painful—not only to the addict, but also to those around the addict—that it is a wonder the addiction is allowed to continue for so long. Why then do addicts wait so long before seeking help for a problem that causes them such grief? It seems so clear to anyone looking on from the outside that addiction is destroying a person and making him or her horribly miserable in the process. Why then do their spouses, lovers and friends wait so long before taking steps to see that they do seek help? A number of factors are frequently at work.

Control

While it may appear that addicts are choosing to continue their self-destructive behavior, the reality is somewhat more complex. Without denying the ultimate responsibility we all have for the choices we make, the fact is that the addiction robs addicts of much of their ability to decide freely and to act in accordance with their decisions. In a sense, it is not really the addict who is in control. The addiction has taken over the driver's seat.

Ironically, the addiction may well have arisen from the individual's attempt to assert control over his or her own emotions. Whenever a woman felt lonely, afraid or angry, she discovered that an interlude of romantic fantasy or sexual behavior made her feel better. This was something new and quite welcome—into the unruly swirl of negative feeling came the sudden ability to make herself feel the way she wanted to feel. The "fix," whatever it was, worked every time. What a marvel! No longer swept along by every wave of disorderly emotion, she could actually control her feelings. But in the end, the device she used to assert control came to assert control over her.

> The social stigma of being a sex addict is great. Sex addicts fear what others would think if they knew of their problem.

Seen in this light, the addict's insistence that he or she is in control of the problem—that the addict can "stop whenever I want to"—is seen for the cruel delusion it is. If the addict is in control, why is his or her career collapsing and marriage disintegrating? Why does the addict so cavalierly cast aside his or her values and principles in reckless pursuit of his or her next "fix"? The fact is that the addiction has taken control; the addict is *out of control*.

Secrecy and Shame

The shame that accompanies people addictions is greater than that among other addictions. In recent years, as the whole area of addiction and recovery has "come out of the closet," much of the stigma of being a recovering alcoholic or drug addict has diminished. It even carries a certain prestige in some trendy circles, but the stigma of being a sex addict is still great. Sex addicts fear what others would think if they knew of their problem. They wince when they think of the host of unpleasant names by which people like them are sometimes called.

Most romance, relationship and sex addicts were shamed by their parents or friends while they were young. This shaming left them feeling worthless—bad about themselves. Such negative emotions, of course, only fuel the addictive process. Addicts gradually resort to more socially unacceptable behaviors, which must be kept hidden, leading to more shame, and so on, in a vicious cycle.

Blame

Blame is, as we have seen, a close partner to shame. It is also a major factor in why the addiction continues. Blaming others is a symptom of a refusal to accept—or even to recognize—one's own responsibility for one's choices and the problems they generate. After all, if the job weren't so stressful, there would be no need for the frequent "breaks" spent at adult bookstores. And that girl walking down the street—look what she is wearing, and the way she is walking! Surely she is being deliberately provocative. How could anyone withstand that?

Such seemingly minor instances of blame shifting eventually lead to wholesale refusal to accept responsibility for the basic challenges and issues of life. Addicts refuse to acknowledge their part in the crumbling of their families, the collapse of their careers and the deterioration of their health.

Denial

Together these factors combine to produce a powerful coping mechanism called denial. Denial is the most prominent factor in keeping addicts addicted. By "denial," I do not simply mean lying to others about what is going on. To be sure, addicts are very deceptive in just this way, but denial goes further. *Denial is a refusal, even an inability, to see and acknowledge the reality of one's situation.* Addicts lie, not only to others, but also to themselves.

Indeed, denial goes even deeper than this. To lie about something, one must be aware of its reality and deliberately choose to misrepresent it. In denial, the addict in effect comes to view reality through a highly selective lens. Addicts become, as it were, unable to see what is happening. They simply do not let reality penetrate their awareness. They repress all feelings that might otherwise serve as indicators that something is wrong. The denial system can become so powerful that even when confronted by a friend with undeniable evidence of their problem, addicts can vehemently deny their actions and not even realize they are lying. There are four main components to a fully functioning denial system.

Redefining Normal. Addicts must maintain the illusion of being in control, in order to fool themselves and others. One of the ways they may do this is by continually redefining what levels of behaviors are "normal" and what levels constitute "a problem." Alcoholics come to believe that drinking a case of beer a day is "normal"—for them. Romance addicts adopt the view that watching four soap operas a day and reading six romance novels a week is also "normal"—for them. Sex addicts attribute their extreme behavior to a "healthy sex drive." In these ways, addicts can assure themselves and those around them that despite outward appearances, there is actually "no problem."

Redefining Reality. Another way addicts deny reality is by redefining it, by persuading themselves that reality is as they want it to be—or, more likely, as their rationalizations require reality to be—rather than as it actually is. The man who places obscene phone calls persuades himself that the women on the other end actually enjoy the experience. The woman who constantly escapes into romantic fantasy, or the man who conducts multiple affairs or visits prostitutes, tells himself or herself that this behavior actually brings new life to his or her marriage.

Blindness. Denial, as we have seen, is unconscious. Indeed, the most pernicious aspect of a denial system is precisely the fact that the addict is unaware of its existence. In effect, the addict denies his or her denial. The familiar anguished cry of the addict's friends and loved ones is, "Can't you see what you're doing to yourself?" To which the addict can only reply, "What in the world are you talking about?"

Deception. Addicts are liars. They lie to those around them to protect their job, their marriage, their reputation. They lie to themselves to protect their self-respect, even their sanity. They lie to cover up past lies, weaving a web of deceit so deep and strong it becomes virtually impenetrable.

Addicts become so skilled at lying, and so dependent on it, that they are unaware they are even doing it. In time, they become virtually incapable of not lying; the practice has been so deeply ingrained in their personality. This is the ultimate denial system, one that can be broken only by the addict "hitting bottom"—hard.

Enablers

The cruelest aspect of addiction—and the final factor that helps addicts stay addicted—is the fact that other people *help* the addiction flourish. They don't mean to, of course. These other people aren't even aware that they are doing it. They may even think they are taking steps to expose and reverse the problem. But in fact they are, in hundreds of little and big ways, enabling the addiction to continue.

Usually, an addict's family is as deeply trapped in denial as the addict him- or herself. Some deny the obvious problem, because they lack the personal strength to confront the reality of an unfaithful husband or an unstable mother. Some deny reality for financial reasons. In effect, they sell out their sanity so that their source of support will not be interrupted.

Others deny the problem for high-minded, even spiritual, reasons. They acknowledge that a problem exists, even that it is costing them their peace of mind, but they believe that it is their duty as a loyal spouse or child to protect the addict, to cover up for him or her. They tell themselves that the addict is just going through a phase, which will soon end. Or they pray that God will cure the addict, so they tell themselves they must simply wait for their prayers to be answered, for their miracle to arrive.

The End of the Line

Addicts will stay addicted until one of several things happens. Their denial system may simply overload and break down. The accumulating shame may crack the wall of deception. Reality may intervene in the form of a lost job, the desertion of a spouse or a deadly disease.

Or someone in the addict's family may step outside the craziness long enough to seek help for himself or herself, eventually forcing the addict to either accept reality or move on.

One way or another, someone or something must break the stalemate or the problem will only get worse. It will not go away by itself. The addiction will grow, and as it does, it will destroy not only the addict, but also all those around him or her. Waiting for the addict to "wake up" can be the longest waiting game on Earth. Often it is the spouse or some other family member who must make the first move if the addict is to have any hope of receiving help.

Addicted to "Love" Characteristics

· Lack of nurturing and attention when young
· Feeling isolated, detached from parents and family
· Outer facade of "having it all together" to hide internal disintegration
· Mistake intensity for intimacy
· Hidden pain
· Seek to avoid rejection and abandonment at all cost
· Afraid to trust anyone in a relationship
· Inner rage over lack of nurturing, early abandonment
· Depressed
· Highly manipulative and controlling of others
· Perceive attraction, attachment and sex as basic human needs, on a par with food and water
· Sense of worthlessness
· Escalating tolerance for high-risk behavior
· Intense need to control self, others, circumstances
· Presence of other addictive or compulsive problems
· Insatiable appetite in area of difficulty
· Using others to alter mood or relieve pain
· Continual questioning of values and lifestyle

- Driven, desperate, frantic personality
- Existence of secret "double life"
- Refusal to acknowledge existence of problem
- Defining out-of-control behavior as normal
- Defining "wants" as "needs"

Note

1. Jean Seligman, "Taking Life One Night at a Time," *Newsweek* (July 20, 1987), p. 49.

CHAPTER 7

Living with Addiction

The familiar, insistent urging began to stir in Ben just as it had so many times before. He felt skittish. He couldn't concentrate on the evening news. He couldn't even bear to face his wife. Ben knew, with awful certainty, what was about to happen. He desperately wanted it not to happen, but felt powerless to prevent it.

Where would it lead this time? What would the consequences be? Ben could not predict. He struggled to contain himself, to force himself to sit in this chair and not give in. But even as he gritted his teeth and tried to rally his will power, Ben knew it was no use. The pressure was mounting to perform some action, some ritual of gratification, which would exorcise the demons of desire and let him return to his senses.

It had started so innocently. For once—for one blessed day—he had felt relatively untroubled by the lust that so frequently besieged him. He had finished dinner and wandered off to the family room, to look through the newspaper, catch the evening news on television, put his feet up, relax.

His eyes flitted back and forth between the sports page and the TV set. A commercial came on, and he turned his thoughts to the baseball scores. The commercial was for women's lingerie. Nothing the least bit racy, but it caught Ben's attention. He lowered the paper and looked intently at the image on the screen. Only a sex addict would know that until very recently, underwear manufacturers could not show real women in their underwear in commercials.

The model was attractive in the sort of conventional, nondescript way that the models in department store catalogs are attractive. The proverbial girl next door—except this one was standing there, smiling, in her underwear. Ben felt a vague flutter in his stomach. He quickly stuck his nose back in the newspaper.

But his mind was no longer on baseball scores. It was on the woman in the commercial. What was she like? Where did she live? Would she be attracted to someone like him? Ben's mind replayed what he had just seen on the television screen. Each time, the model's figure grew more sensuous, her eyes more seductive and inviting.

Ben rubbed his eyes and gave his head a toss, trying to shake himself out of his reverie. But it was too late. Images of other women began to crowd into his mind, women he had seen in magazines and movies and adult nightclubs, images of what they had looked like and what they had done and the ways they had done it.

Now the woman in the television commercial was one of them, the images swirling in his mind, stirring his feelings, exciting his memory, putting his whole nervous system on edge, inflaming his desire for . . . what? He wasn't exactly sure. But whatever it was, he suddenly knew he had to have it, now.

Ben got up from his easy chair and made his way to the kitchen, where his wife Donna was finishing up the dinner dishes. He went to the cupboard and got a glass, and then went to the refrigerator for the milk. He took a sip and then spoke.

"I'm going to have to run down to the office for a couple hours tonight, hon. There's some work I've got to have done by tomorrow morning."

Donna had heard such statements before. She didn't believe him, but she had no solid basis on which to challenge him. She knew he wasn't really planning to go to the office. She had a pretty clear idea where he *was* going. There had been telltale signs: receipts from adult bookstores in his pockets, the smell of smoke and perfume on his clothes. She had tried dozens of times, in these situations, to dissuade him from leaving, had begged him to stay home, to spend more time with her and the children. She knew it was useless. He was going to go no matter what she said.

"Well, try not to work too late," she finally replied. "It's your turn to drive the kids' carpool in the morning."

"Okay," Ben said. He put his glass down by the sink, gave his wife a quick peck on the cheek and went out the side door into the garage.

Donna heard the car start as she rinsed the glass and put it in the top rack of the dishwasher. In spite of herself, she wondered where he was headed, and how long he would be gone this time. When he finally came home on nights like this, he was *different* somehow—more distant, more aloof, but somehow more attentive and affectionate, all at the same time. As though he were trying to make up to her for something.

But make up for what? Was there another woman? Or was he really spending all this time in one of *those* places? Donna shuddered at the thought. She had seen the ads for the bookstores and nightclubs, and had driven past them on the rare occasions when she had to go to that part of the city. She had read in the paper of the kinds of things that happened in that part of town: the drugs, the crime, the prostitution. What if Ben . . .

She didn't let her mind complete that thought. Donna almost hoped there was another woman. It would be easier to deal with that than the thought that her husband of 12 years was going out nights and . . .

Again she stopped short. It was too much to think about. A thousand questions raced through her mind. What kinds of trouble might her husband be getting into? What kinds of risks might he be running? Of getting mugged? Or getting some awful disease? What might the consequences be?

Donna felt sick to her stomach. What was wrong with him? What was wrong with her? What was missing in their marriage that he had to go elsewhere to seek gratification? Why did she let him go out? Why didn't she stop him somehow?

But she couldn't stop him. Hadn't she tried everything? Pleading? Anger? Tears? She had even tried acting super sexy, enticing him to stay with her. But that only made her feel cheap, as though she, his wife, were suddenly no better than one of . . . one of them.

Donna didn't know what to do. But she knew she had to do something. She couldn't live this way any more, listening to her husband lie to her, watching him go out at night to betray her. She was afraid for him, for herself, for the children. Her resolve stiffened. Somehow, she was going to force this whole crazy business to come to a stop.

Meanwhile, Ben slowly cruised through the dark downtown streets. This was a trip he had made numerous times in the past year or so. Each trip had started with some small spark igniting the compulsions that lay dormant within. A television commercial, a picture in a catalog or on a billboard, a woman passing on the street—virtually anything, it seemed, could serve as a trigger.

Once that happened, the rest of the process seemed virtually preordained. Before long he would be driving these same streets to this same section of downtown, where women in ludicrous outfits slumped against the brick buildings, waiting for a potential customer to drive by.

Ben checked out the women on both sides of the street, looking for one who sparked his interest. He also kept an eye out for police cars lurking in the side streets. The cops were seldom so obvious as to bring a regular patrol car through the area. Ben had learned to spot the unmarked cars: The plain, late-model sedans with blackwall tires, lights off, motors running, parked in between the areas lit by the street lamps. He didn't see any cars tonight.

As he drove by, the women looked back at him. Some of them smiled, even waved, trying to encourage him to stop. He didn't like the ones who did that. He found their eagerness distasteful.

He turned around and headed back up to the end of the street where he had started. There was a party store there, a dirty little shop that sold liquor, cigarettes and magazines. He paused briefly and thumbed through some of the porn magazines, then went to the counter and bought a package of condoms for "protection."

As he opened the door to leave, he heard the cashier call to him, "Hey, mister!" Ben froze. What had he done? A thousand wild, improbable thoughts raced through his mind. Had he done something wrong? Did the man recognize him? He turned and looked back toward the counter.

"Yes?"

"Want your change?"

"Oh. Oh, yeah. Thanks. Wasn't thinking."

"I mean, if you don't want it, I'd be glad to start a collection with it, hey?"

"No, that's fine. I mean, yeah, thanks. Thanks."

Ben's heart was pounding and he felt dizzy. He grabbed the change and hurried to the door. The cashier shook his head and smirked. Ben had a good idea what the guy was thinking.

He pulled out of the parking lot and resumed his slow cruising. Earlier he had noticed a girl, one he had been with before. She had been on the next block down. There she was. He could feel the adrenaline starting to pump now, the familiar rush of excitement. He pulled over to the curb where she was standing with another girl. He looked at her and nodded. She pushed away from the building and walked slowly toward his car.

She was young, maybe 18, with long hair that looked like a cheap wig, short skirt, too much makeup. Ben reached across the seat and rolled down the window. She leaned on the door on folded arms and looked in at him.

"Whatcha lookin' for?" she asked.

"You know," he answered. "A date. Let's go."

"Not so fast," she said. "Maybe I got other plans. You gonna make it worth my while?"

"Yeah, sure," Ben said. "How about 50 bucks? That make it worth your while?"

"You're offering me 50 bucks to go on a date with you? Where we goin', the movies? You must have something more in mind." She smiled coyly as she said it and leaned further inside the car.

For crying out loud, Ben thought. *What's this all about? We both know what's going on. Why does she want to play games!* He smiled back. "Yeah, I got something more in mind." He mentioned what it was.

She opened the door and slid onto the seat next to him. "Great," she said. "Let's go."

Ben shifted the car into drive. There was a seedy motel down the street where you could rent rooms by the hour. He started to pull away from the curb.

An instant later, bright lights appeared in his rearview mirror, a car slammed on its brakes right behind him and a voice on a loudspeaker told him to stay in his car. *Oh, my God,* Ben thought. *Police! Where had they come from?*

Dazed, he turned to look at the girl next to him. She showed him the tiny microphone hidden in her halter top. "Sorry, mister," she shrugged. "It was either you or me tonight. My kid needs me at home, not in jail." She climbed out of the car, handed the microphone to the officer and walked away.

Donna felt sick to her stomach. What was wrong with him? What was wrong with her? What was missing in their marriage that Ben had to go elsewhere to seek gratification?

Ben had seen hundreds of TV cop shows where suspects were made to spread their legs and lean against their cars, arms out flat across the hood, while policemen frisked them. But this was no TV show. This was real. As one of the officers wrenched his hands behind his back and put the handcuffs on his wrists, the other spoke to him in a flat, monotone voice, "You are under arrest. You have the right to remain silent . . . "

Under arrest. The words seemed to stab him like an ice pick. He was under arrest! He, Ben, a married man, with two cars and a house and a family under arrest! For soliciting a prostitute on the street!

His head was swimming as he imagined what would happen next. He would go "downtown," as the TV cops always called it. He would be thrown into some small, horrible room with God knows what kind of awful people. He would stand before a judge, in handcuffs, hearing his name and the charge read out loud. Who might be there to hear it? Were there reporters there at this hour? Would it all be in the papers the next day? What would people think?

Waves of shame and anguish washed over him as he imagined his co-workers, his boss, people in his church and even his children seeing his name in the paper, reading with shocked disbelief what he had done. He sat in stunned silence as the police car made its way to the station. *Under arrest, under arrest, under arrest*, replayed in his mind.

Donna was lying in bed reading when the call came. She picked up the phone on the second ring.

"Hello, Donna?"

"Ben? Is that you?"

"Yeah. Listen. Donna, I'm in trouble."

"What kind of trouble?"

"Trouble with the police."

A sick, sinking feeling came over her, a sudden realization that her life was about to be changed. Every inch of her body felt like a tender wound. She was paralyzed by the sensation that she was now, at last, living through a life-shattering moment she had known all along must come. She realized that in her husband's next breath would be revealed the secrets that had left her wondering in fear these past few years. The seed of Ben's restlessness was about to be uncovered.

Donna lay very still on the bed, barely conscious of anything but the telephone receiver cradled against her ear. She stared at the ceiling and asked, very calmly, "What did you do?"

"Well, look, I'll explain it when you get here, okay?"

"What did *you* do?" There was an unmistakable edge in her voice this time.

Ben tried to think of a way to soften the force, the anger, revealed in her voice. Before he could think of anything else to say, he blurted out the truth.

"I got picked up for soliciting. Soliciting a prostitute." He waited. There was no reply, just Donna's steady breathing on the other end.

"Look, it's all a mistake. An incredible mistake. I can tell you about it when you come down." Still no reply. Was she weeping? Angry? In shock? He had no way of telling.

"Listen, Donna, you've got to come down here and get me, okay? And bring some money. I'm going to need some money for bail. So bring the cash in my sock drawer, okay? Donna?"

Donna still lay in bed. She hadn't moved. She picked up the corner of her robe's tie. She turned it this way and that, examining it intently, as if it were the most crucial item in the universe right now. She brought it to her mouth and bit down on it with every ounce of strength she could muster. Then she relaxed, took a deep breath, stared back at the ceiling and spoke to her husband very slowly and distinctly.

"I'm not coming to get you."

"You're what?" He practically screamed at her. "Donna, look. I told you, it's all a mistake. Now you've got to come down here and . . . "

"No, Ben." She was amazed at how calm, how utterly steady, her voice sounded. "I'm not coming. I'm not going to bail you out of jail."

"But Donna . . . "

"Ben, listen to me." She felt anger rising up from deep inside her, like a wave about to crest on shore. "You got yourself in there, you get yourself out. And when you do, don't come back here. I don't care where you go, just don't come here. I'll send your clothes and things over to your mother's."

"Donna, how can you do this?" Ben's voice was pleading now, like a little boy's. "I need you. You won't even let me explain. This is all just a terrible mistake."

"I'm sorry, Ben," she choked through her tears. The anger had subsided now, replaced by a wave of bitter grief. "I knew something was pulling you away from me. Away from us. I knew you were doing something. I guess I knew all along what it was. I just didn't want to face it.

But I can't go through any more of this. It's over, Ben. It's over. I can't let you come back here. Not now."

She was sobbing. "Maybe later. Maybe after you've had time to go to work on yourself. You get your life together and then maybe we can talk. But not now."

She took a breath and wiped her eyes with the corner of her robe. "I'm not coming to get you, Ben. I'm not going to do anything to make this any easier for you."

Before he could get another word in, she hung up.

Ben's call had been like a wrecking ball, crashing through every wall of denial she had built up to try to preserve her marriage, her family, her sense of dignity. Two little words had done it: "police" and "prostitute." Those two words summed up the awful confirmation of her worst fears. She had hoped she was wrong, even as she knew—somehow just knew—that she was not.

Donna had refused to face it. She had turned her eyes and refused to see what had been staring her in the face all along: all the mysterious absences, the explanations that didn't add up, the telltale signs whose full meaning she would not let herself accept.

And now this. Donna felt relieved in a way. At least something had *happened.* The game was over. It was out in the open—what they were dealing with. No, what *he* was dealing with. Ben had to be the one to fix what was broken. Others would criticize her, she supposed, for deserting him in his dark hour of need, but somehow she knew it was his only hope. Forcing him to face his crisis on his own, without shielding him from it or cushioning the impact, was the best thing she could do for him, hard as it was. It was the way for her to love him now.

Donna got up and went to the children. She knelt beside each one and said a prayer, that through this ordeal they would all be made stronger. She kissed each one, gently, so as not to wake them. Then she went back to her room. There was going to be so much to do. But not now. Now she needed to rest.

Donna slipped her robe off and crawled into bed, alone. The moment she closed her eyes, her mind was suddenly flooded with doubts and fears. Every disaster, every conceivable calamity, played itself out in her imagination. She tossed and turned for what seemed like hours. Finally, she grew weary from dreading her new reality and fell into a restless slumber. It seemed only minutes later that the sunlight creeping through the window awakened her. It was a new day. Time to face the awesome task of living through this nightmare.

Sacrifices on the Altar of Addiction

Ben and Donna paid a high price for their problem. Ben was addicted to sex, and Donna was addicted to her relationship with him—until that one night when everything came crashing down on both of them.

Addiction is never cheap. It is a thief. It robs its victims—of everything. Many people pay the price for years without stopping to realize just how much it really costs them. Facing the cost of addiction squarely can be the first step from the prison of obsession and compulsion back to freedom.

In recovery, people addicts invariably look back on their lives and lament that they accomplished so little and had so little time for things that really mattered.

The altar of addiction requires tremendous sacrifice. In the worship of romance, relationships or sex—which is, as we have seen, ultimately the worship of self—the addict will pay a dear price. God, family, time, reputation, job, self-respect—in time, all of these will be handed over to the addiction idol. The search for instant gratification is all that matters. Nothing else matters. Anything that blocks the path to relief inevitably is seen as dispensable.

Lost Time
One of the most valuable assets lost right from the beginning is time.

Obsessive thinking drains away hours of productive time. The rituals of the hunt and entrapment steal time from family, work and the pursuit of positive self-development. Everything else is placed on hold while the addict tracks down his or her fix. In recovery, people addicts invariably look back on their lives and lament that they accomplished so little and had so little time for things that really mattered.

Lost time is a part of the price of addiction that is often overlooked, but it is a heavy cost indeed, because it can never be reclaimed. Reputations can be rehabilitated. Relationships can be restored. Trust can be reestablished. But time, once squandered, is lost forever.

Ruined Reputation

One's good name is a precious commodity to sacrifice on the altar of addiction. The word "cheap" is frequently used when describing the reputation of romance, relationship or sex addicts. Addicts typically struggle with their self-image anyway. The additional burden of a self-inflicted bad reputation only makes matters that much worse.

A reputation can be restored, but it is seldom easy. It can take years and a great deal of effort. Tragically, some never have the chance to try, because they start counting the cost too late.

Shattered Self-Respect

Self-respect is not easily surrendered. All addicts have a behavioral "line" that they believe they must not cross. As long as they stay on this side of the line, they feel their self-respect is intact. But sooner or later, unchecked addiction pushes the addict across the line.

Initially, addicts deal with this blow by drawing a new line, one that they tell themselves is more realistic. When that line is crossed, they draw yet another. All the time, they reassure themselves that everything is under control. They can handle it.

In time, the addiction reels out of control, and *every* line is crossed, almost before the addict realizes what is happening. What addicts once detested, they now find themselves doing. What they once swore to avoid, they now seek out.

With each episode, their self-respect suffers another blow. And as self-respect deteriorates, the motivation to engage in destructive behavior increases, and the restraint on such behavior diminishes. Life becomes a vicious circle of self-defeat.

Emotional Turmoil

Addiction exacts a severe emotional toll. Addicts are haunted by guilt, fear and anger. Addicts feel guilty over what they have done, what they have become and the people they have hurt. Sometimes the guilt drives them back to their addictive behavior—the only salve they know for pain.

Addicts are overwhelmed by fear. They fear being found out. They fear losing control. They fear going crazy. They fear for their very lives. The fear blocks out the ability to perceive reality correctly and to think clearly, opening the way to more addictive behavior.

Addicts are filled with anger. They are angry with those they blame for causing their problems. At the same time, they are angry with themselves for not being able to stop doing things that cause them such grief.

Physical Effects

Addiction leads to physical illness and dysfunction. The stress of leading an isolated, secretive, double life is often manifested in stomach problems, neck and back pain, headaches and sleeplessness. The pressure of guilt accelerates the aging process; inner turmoil frequently makes addicts appear 10 years older than they are.

This is to say nothing of the more obvious physical consequences that can follow when the addiction involves sexual behavior. Chlamydia, genital warts, herpes, gonorrhea, syphilis vaginids, hepatitis, AIDS—all of these diseases and more confront those trapped in people addictions.

Marriage and Family

As the story of Ben and Donna illustrates, one of the main casualties of addiction is often the addict's marriage and family life. This is perhaps the crudest cost of all, because it is exacted not only from the addicts themselves, but also from those who love them.

Witness the guilt, the fear, the loss of self-respect suffered by Donna just wondering what her husband's problem might be—let alone the loneliness and economic strain that befell her when he left, and the dislocation to the children caused by their father's disappearance.

The high cost of addiction gives rise to obvious questions: How can those involved with the addicted learn how to recognize their problems? How can they help the addict seek the help he or she needs?

The High Cost of Addiction

· Time lost from family, work, other pursuits
· Tarnished reputation
· Shattered self-respect
· Financial burdens: money spent on pornography, prostitution, new clothing and so on
· Emotional strain
· Physical consequences: exhaustion, stress (manifested in stomach problems, neck and back pain, headaches, sleeplessness), unwanted pregnancy, sexually transmitted diseases
· Family dislocation: estrangement from spouse and children, separation, divorce, children grow up vulnerable to same addiction
· Job loss
· Alienation of friends
· Legal consequences

Red Flags of Sex Addiction

When partners of sex addicts think back, most can remember numerous instances that were red flags. They may, for example, have come across unusual belongings: pornography, articles of women's clothing, suspicious receipts, perfume or other gift items or sexual paraphernalia of various kinds. When confronted with these items, addicts explain them away with some plausible rationalization. Addicts may even try to persuade their spouse that "the real problem" is their own overreaction to something "harmless."

Along with the hard evidence may come less tangible indicators: unexplained absences and late hours, or inconsistencies regarding where the addicts were and for how long. Typically, the addicted partners will try to "cover" for these blunders with extra attention, gifts, flattery and so on. They may even admit to minor indiscretions, trying to create the impression of an open, honest relationship—while in fact covering up more serious breaches.

Those living in a close relationship with someone addicted to sex are almost always surrounded by signs of their addicted partner's secret, double life. Yet their denial prevents them from seeing what is before their very eyes.

Going back further, before the marriage or relationship even started, it may become clear that the individual was hiding something from the outset. There may be signs that the relationship itself was part of the addict's attempts to cope with his or her problem. Addicts often hope that a stable relationship will provide the "cure" they need. As some of the case histories in earlier chapters have illustrated, this is a vain hope.

Evidence of a Double Life

· Unusual items (pornography, suspicious receipts, sexual paraphernalia and so on)
· Unexplained absences, late hours, tardiness
· Inconsistencies as to times, places and so on
· Outright falsehoods
· Periods of disinclination to have sex with partner
· Overly "wonderful" treatment

There are more serious forms of marital dysfunction that can occur when one of the partners is addicted to sex. One of these occurs when the addicted husband attempts to act out his addiction with his spouse, pressuring her to be sexual in ways that make her uncomfortable. When she finally refuses to compromise her values, or even comes to resent and avoid sex altogether, the husband uses this as a pretext to justify seeking gratification in other places. He tells himself that he cannot help it. His needs are not being met at home, so he must look elsewhere—all the time conveniently overlooking the fact that it was his own manipulative behavior that created the situation.

Or almost the precise opposite situation may arise. The sex-addicted husband places his wife on a pedestal, as it were, holding her "above that sort of thing," never placing any sexual demands on her at all. This is sometimes called the Madonna-whore complex, in which the male grotesquely bifurcates his image of womanhood. On the one hand is the pure virgin, with whom he is gallant and chaste. On the other is the sensuous temptress, with whom he acts out his most wanton fantasies.

These are, admittedly, extreme cases—though they are seen regularly at most treatment centers. Still, as distasteful as they are, behind each one is a wounded person crying for help—and often trying, even against his or her conscious will, to be found out.

As hard as addicts work to maintain the secrecy of their double lives, they also long to end the guilt, shame and hopelessness caused by their behavior. Beneath the compulsion and deceit remains a human soul yearning for wholeness. The trail of evidence is often meant, however unconsciously, to bring about revelation, confrontation, admission, confession, acceptance and recovery.

An Unconscious Cry for Help

· To end a double life
· To stop the guilt and shame
· To prompt confrontation and confession
· To attain wholeness and reconciliation

To the Wives of Sex Addicts

There may be no lonelier group of people on Earth than the spouses of sex addicts. Usually, these are women who either know or suspect that their husbands are involved in behavior they can neither stomach nor comprehend. What makes it worse is that there seems to be no one they can talk to. Most cities have dozens of support groups for spouses of alcoholics or drug addicts, and the stigma attached to attending such groups has greatly diminished in recent years.

Not so with sex addiction. The only person who feels greater shame than the sex addict himself is often the addict's wife. The very nature of the problem seems to implicate her as a contributing factor—surely if she were "woman enough," her man would not need to "have his needs met" elsewhere. This line of thinking is a cruel lie, and it places innumerable women under a tremendous burden of guilt, preventing them from seeking the counsel and support they so badly need.

Here are a few words of advice, then, for wives whose husbands are trapped in sex addiction.

Men and Women

First, take to heart the first lesson you learned in your high school health class: In terms of sexual response, men and women are very different creatures. For women, sex is intimately interwoven with intimacy, tenderness, stability and commitment in a relationship. It is, indeed, the ultimate expression of these things. To be sure, women do experience sexual desire and gratification at the physiological level. But it is seldom divorced from these more relational and spiritual aspects.

In men, this distinction is far more common. Men can and do experience a craving for intimacy and commitment; they can and do view sex as an expression of these things. But male sexual response can also be readily detached from other considerations and become a psychological and physiological drive in and of itself.

Sense stimuli that leave women relatively unaffected—erotic pictures, to take an obvious example—can have a powerful and immediate effect on men. This is neither good nor bad in itself, but it is a significant difference

that women need to understand and accept even if they cannot fully identify with it.

Love and Lust

Closely linked to this male-female difference is the distinction between
love and lust. Love is personal; lust is impersonal. Love is concrete,
focused on a particular object; lust is unfocused, capable of fixing on
almost any available object. Love tends toward faithfulness; lust is a wan-
derer. Love seeks stability; lust is short-lived and mercurial. Love is an
affair of the mind and heart; lust is an affair of the emotions and the
hormones. Love is a matter of giving; lust is a matter of taking.

Women, as well as men, are capable of both love and lust. However,
men seem far more prone to experience lust than women and to experience it more intensely and more uncontrollably. This explains why the
majority of sex addicts are men. Sex addiction, in a sense, is really lust
addiction. Lust is the engine that fuels the addictive behavior.

This in turn explains why men often see no contradiction between
loving their wives on the one hand and lusting after pictures of nude
women, or even prostitutes, on the other. They experience the two as separate and distinct experiences; neither seems to interfere with the other.
Thus, what for women are inseparably intertwined—love and sex—can
seem to occupy two entirely separate niches of the male psyche.

"Woman Enough"

Understanding the way men detach lust from love helps free a wife from
the most agonizing prison of all: the false belief that her husband's sex
addiction is somehow her fault, that if she were only thinner, prettier,
more glamorous, more responsive or more wanton in bed, her husband's
need for sex would be satisfied. Many wives live under a crushing burden
of guilt, believing that it is their inadequacy as women, as wives or as
lovers that has made their husbands sexually compulsive.

For many men, and especially for male sex addicts, love and lust are
like two different appetites, satisfied in two different ways. Many wives
believe that if they treat their husbands better, or have intercourse with
them more regularly, the husband's addictive drives will be satisfied.

This is like expecting an alcoholic to be satisfied by drinking more water. It doesn't work.

The alcoholic's problem is not thirst; it is not solved merely by drinking liquid. Rather, it is alcohol that both fuels and satisfies the compulsion. In the same way, it is not merely sex but lust that fuels addictive behavior. The male sex addict can enjoy a wonderfully tender and satisfying sexual relationship with his wife, and then be on the prowl for lustful encounters later the same day.

The message to wives is simple: You are not the cause of your husband's addiction, and you cannot be the cure. The problem is in him, and it is there that the battle must be fought and won.

Education

It is vitally important that the wife of a sex addict—or any addict, for that matter—seek to learn all she can about her husband's particular problem. Only in this way will she be able to protect herself from the guilt that comes from faulty understanding. Only in this way will she be able to help her husband find wholeness. Only in this way will she be able to guard herself from more heartache in the meantime.

Reading this book is an excellent place to begin the educational process. Other materials, listed in the resources at the end of this book, provide more detailed insight into particular aspects of the problem.

Self-Care

From education flows a clear understanding of how the wife can take proper care of her own well-being. Many wives, on the theory that they are supposed to sacrifice themselves for their husbands, tolerate terrible mental and emotional anguish, and even physical abuse.

This is not what the Bible means by self-sacrifice. To sacrifice your life for your spouse means sometimes to lay down your own desires and preferences for the sake of what is best for him. It does not mean to subject yourself to abuse for the sake of your spouse's sickness. Genuine, loving self-sacrifice *requires* an appropriate level of self-care.

Self-care begins with the resolute awareness that the problem is in your husband, not in you; that you did not cause his problem and you cannot cure it; and that his sickness is not your fault. Keeping clear on these fundamental truths is crucial to maintaining your sanity.

Self-care also involves not compromising your values and principles to feed his addiction—for example, by being pressured into sexual behavior you find repugnant. And self-care emphatically includes not subjecting yourself to the threat of disease or to physical abuse at the hands of a sex addict, even if he is your husband.

Support Groups

Most wives, if they are going to follow through consistently on healthy self-care, will require support from others who have been there and know what they are going through. Living with an addict who is acting out his disease can literally be enough to make you crazy. Strong, reliable support is a must.

Most areas have treatment centers, counseling centers or telephone hotlines where people struggling with a live-in addict can go for professional assistance. An increasing number of areas have support groups for the spouses of sex addicts. If no such group is listed by name in your area, try visiting a meeting of Alcoholics Anonymous. Many of the basic concepts of living with an alcoholic can be applied to living with a sex addict. Whatever form it takes, if you are married to an addict and trying to handle it on your own, don't. Seek help. You don't need to face it alone.

Tough Love

What about helping the addict? Learning to cope with his problem more effectively is important. Doesn't the ultimate solution lie in helping him pursue recovery?

Indeed, it does. But all the foregoing steps—understanding, education, self-care and peer support—are prerequisites to learning how to help the addict in the most effective way possible. Recovering codependents call it "tough love." Simply put, it means having the strength to relate to the addict in ways that will expedite, rather than retard, his coming face-to-face with the reality of his situation.

This means, primarily, not being an *enabler*. As the name suggests, an enabler is one who, by his or her attitudes and actions, makes it possible for an addict to continue acting out behind the wall of denial.

How Wives of Sex Addicts Act as Enablers

· They ignore the signs of their husbands' double lives.
· They accede to their husbands' unhealthy sexual demands.
· They tolerate abusive behavior toward themselves or their children.
· They place themselves at risk of serious disease.
· They cover up for their husbands' behavior by lying or making excuses for him to bosses, coworkers, friends and family.

Eventually, every sex addict's wife must come to the place that Donna came to: where she allows her husband's denial to be shattered and courageously demands that he face his problem himself. Once this has happened, there is much she can do to be helpful and supportive of his recovery. But until then, such "helpful and supportive" behavior is probably nothing more than *enabling* behavior, which helps to strengthen the wall of denial rather than to demolish it.

Runaway Addicts

The cost of addiction is high. Too often addicts and those around them fail to acknowledge it until it has mounted too high. They race faster and faster down the avenue of addiction. Addicts convince themselves that they are in control, that they can stop any time they want. But by the time addicts truly see the need to stop, they realize they are in a runaway vehicle with no brakes. Only when addicts run head-on into something immovable—the law, a disease, public humiliation—do they come to a crashing halt.

And, yet, it does not *have* to be this way. There is another avenue addicts, and their loved ones, can take. It is called recovery.

Recovery: From the Bottom Up

Sooner or later, the addict hits bottom. "Bottom" is the last place the addict expects to arrive. The psychological dynamics of addiction persuade an addict that he or she will be the exception, the one who breaks the inevitable pattern. The addict will be able to ride the winds of attraction, attachment or lust, and never come down. But eventually, by one route or another, the addict always does.

When an addict hits bottom, it feels like—and usually is—the darkest moment of his or her life. Different individuals hit bottom in different ways and at different points. Some lose their job. Their husbands or wives leave them. Some discover they have contracted a disease.

Whatever the precise circumstances may be, the stark, brutal fact of the matter is that for that person, at that moment, the game is up. The alibis run out. The excuses fail. The lies surface. The addict crashes head-on with reality, and the thick shell of denial is finally shattered.

But for all its misery, hitting bottom is also a *hopeful* experience. The reason: When you are at the bottom, there is nowhere to go but up. Anything is better than remaining in that place of desolation. When the addict hits bottom, the addict may finally resolve to break the cycle that has enslaved him or her to his or her passions.

These are not the empty promises that characterize the typical addiction cycle. From the vantage point of "bottom," addicts finally see the terrible reality of their situation and make the momentous decision to change. Knowing they have made hollow resolutions before, they take action on their decision.

Knowing that they cannot afford the luxury of procrastination, they take action now. They pick up the phone and call the doctor, the treatment center, the minister, the support group—the number they may have known all along they must dial if they are to make any meaningful progress. They break through the self-imprisonment of denial, take a deep breath and take the step they have been resisting for so long. With that single step, they begin the painful, joyful journey known as recovery.

Principles of Recovery

People often ask what a treatment center does to help people move out of their problems and into recovery. The answer is surprisingly simple—so much so that it can frustrate people who like to make life more complicated than it actually needs to be. Addicts are frequently like that. Their insistence on overintellectualizing and overconceptualizing recovery is often nothing more than a subtle evasion tactic.

Are You Ready for Recovery?

1. Are you ready to change?
2. How bad will it have to get before you *are* ready?
3. At what point would you admit you are out of control?
4. How much pain are you willing to endure for the sake of your problem?

5. How much are you prepared to lose in the pursuit of your addiction?
6. Are you comfortable with your life as it is, or would you like to see a change?
7. Would your life be better or worse without your addiction?
8. What would you be willing to do to get free?
9. When will enough be enough? After five years of agony? After the collapse of your career? Your marriage? Your family?
10. Are you comfortable with the prospect of a life lived in isolation from others? Even from God?

What most treatment centers do is simple, but effective. It works. It helps the depressed romance addict to acknowledge reality and function normally again. It motivates the relationship addict to abandon false and destructive attachments, and learn to build authentic, loving relationships. It enables the sex addict to rise above the domination of lust and grow toward sexual health. It enables all addicts to deal squarely with the underlying problems that drive their addictions and to learn the way to genuine intimacy and personal wholeness.

The principles of recovery are based on sound principles of spiritual growth, psychology and therapy. They are lived out through the Twelve Steps, a practical program of recovery pioneered by Alcoholics Anonymous and now modified for use with a wide range of addictive and compulsive problems.

The Twelve Steps make the addict the prime human agent in his or her own recovery. The addict doesn't wait for the doctor, the counselor or the therapist to "fix" his or her problems. Rather, with God's help, the addict takes the steps that will lead to wholeness. The Twelve Steps help open an addict's mind, heart and will to a living faith and a daily reliance on God, whom he or she recognizes as the source of life and wholeness.

Five basic principles are important to keep in mind. Everything that happens in treatment supports and enhances these five principles: acceptance, confession, forgiveness, accountability and love. Together, these five principles form the foundation of recovery.

Benefits of Recovery

1. Experience genuine love
2. Discover true intimacy
3. Fill the aching void inside
4. Grasp the meaning of life
5. Find union with God

I have witnessed some marvelous instances of recovery over the years—each of them proof that the power to change is available if and when we humbly and honestly invite God into our lives. I remember a pastor who had been in bondage to pornography and masturbation for his entire adult life—including his 20 years in the ministry. One day, he was watching a television talk show about sex addiction. The description of the signs and symptoms of addiction hit him right between the eyes. In that moment, a tiny crack opened up in the wall of denial he had been building for so long.

This man was instantly convinced that he needed to seek help. He called a treatment center on the spot and began treatment that very day. He made the most of each day. Layer after layer of denial was stripped away as he came to see the reality of his problem.

The craziness and selfishness of addiction were replaced with responsibility and self-respect. He became a more other-centered person, filled with love and eager to make amends to those he had hurt. After he left the treatment center and went back home, he joined a support group and began helping others recover from their addictions. He has since returned to his church and resumed his ministry. That man exemplifies how the following principles of recovery work.

Acceptance

Acceptance is the first principle of recovery. Recovery begins when an individual moves from denial to acceptance. It does not happen all at once, and it is not something that another person can do for the individual suffering from an addiction. Still, each time we confront a person with reality, we help bring the addict closer to accepting his or her situation and seeing the need to change.

Most people have lived in denial for years before they come for help. Often, they have been surrounded by "coconspirators," who have enabled their dysfunctional behavior to continue, and who have reinforced their denial system. Together, they have constructed a delusional world where the full extent of the problem is never acknowledged, let alone dealt with. The first job of treatment, then—and the first step toward recovery—is to bring someone to the point of acceptance.

You Know There's a Problem When . . .

- Something doesn't feel right
- You've been groping for answers
- You want things to change
- Others have mentioned or hinted at a problem
- You feel badly about the way you treat other people
- You are tired of fighting alone
- Things are getting worse, not better
- You sense you are losing control

Sometimes people ask if a person can be helped who does not want help. Usually, what they are really asking is whether they should wait until that person asks for help, or whether there is something they can do to help the process along.

Ultimately, we cannot help someone who refuses to be helped. As the old saying goes "addiction is an inside job." Addiction can only be cured from the inside—by the addict taking the necessary steps to recover. If a person had a purely physical problem, like the flu, it would theoretically be possible to force medicine into his or her system against the person's will and thereby make him or her get better.

But for all its physiological components, addiction is also a psychological, emotional and even spiritual condition. It requires the active complicity of the addict in order to continue, and it requires the active cooperation of the addict in order to move toward recovery.

There is something we can do for addicts who don't want help. We can stop being enablers and start being people who aggressively confront them with reality and force them to confront it as well. We can lovingly, but persistently, hold up the mirror of reality and make them see themselves as they really are, driving away the illusions and deceptions in which they try to take refuge.

I have had the good fortune to see many people move from denial to acceptance. You can be sure this crucial shift happens once addicts are able to confess their problem to other people. This is the ultimate sign that they are no longer primarily invested in perpetuating their elaborate denial system; instead, they are bringing their problem into the light where it can be dealt with.

I have seen floods of tears follow this leap into self-awareness and vulnerability. I have even seen people collapse as they tore down the walls of isolation and allowed others into their world of pain. Nothing is more moving than to watch addicts abandon their illusions and defenses, even in the face of a brutal reality. And nothing is more healing than for addicts to be welcomed into a circle of loving, supportive people who know what they are going through because they have been there themselves.

Powerlessness. Acceptance is built on the foundation of recognizing our own powerlessness. We spend so much of our lives trying to prove, to ourselves as well as to others, how strong we are, how capable we are, how "together" we are. The battle cry of addicts is "I can handle it." In their weakness, addicts try to compensate and prove their strength to others all the more. But the harder they try, the more the addiction fights back and overwhelms them.

Even as we attempt to hide our weakness, God invites us to use our weakness to open ourselves to His power. It is when we are weak—and when we accept that we are weak—that God can be strong in us and unleash His power in our lives.

The First Step to recovery is always the same. We must be able to say, and believe, that we are powerless over our problem and that our lives have become unmanageable because of it. We need to give up trying to make ourselves better by our own strength and wisdom, and surrender to the fact that apart from the power of God, we cannot hope to conquer the problem that has so ruthlessly conquered us.

The power we need can come only from God. It does not reside in any human being, and we cannot manufacture it. Yet, this power is readily available, just for the asking.

In the Bible, the apostle Paul writes about the relationship between weakness and strength. No one would ordinarily want to be weak, but Paul says that God's view of the matter is different:

> "My grace is sufficient for you, for my power is made perfect in weakness." Therefore I will boast all the more gladly about my weaknesses, so that Christ's power may rest on me. . . . For when I am weak, then I am strong" (2 Cor. 12:9-10).

The Twelve Steps of Sex and Love Addicts Anonymous

1. Admitted we were powerless over sex and love addiction—that our lives had become unmanageable.
2. Came to believe that a Power greater than ourselves could restore us to sanity.
3. Made a decision to turn our will and our lives over to the care of God as we understood God.
4. Made a searching and fearless moral inventory of ourselves.
5. Admitted to God, to ourselves, and to another human being the exact nature of our wrongs.
6. Were entirely ready to have God remove all these defects of character.
7. Humbly asked God to remove our shortcomings.
8. Made a list of all persons we had harmed, and became willing to make amends to them all.

9. Made direct amends to such people wherever possible, except when to do so would injure them or others.

10. Continued to take personal inventory and when we were wrong, promptly admitted it.

11. Sought through prayer and meditation to improve our conscious contact with a Power greater than ourselves, praying only for knowledge of God's will for us and the power to carry that out.

12. Having had a spiritual awakening as a result of these steps, we tried to carry this message to sex and love addicts, and to practice these principles in all areas of our lives.[1]

Pages 67-68, reprinted from the Basic Text of Sex and Love Addicts Anonymous, Copyright 1986 with permission of The Augustine Fellowship, Sex and Love Addicts Anonymous, Fellowship-Wide Services, Inc.

This paradox points to the radical redirection of life that occurs when people begin the recovery process. They go from avoiding even the appearance of weakness, from covering up their limitations and denying their defects, to openly accepting their weaknesses in order that God's power may be at work in them. To accept weakness in this way is to step down from the throne, to climb off the pedestal of ego, to refuse to play God any longer. This admission of utter powerlessness opens the door for God to be in control of their lives.

Not surprisingly, this kind of acceptance and admission of powerlessness is harder to achieve where the stigma of the problem is greater. Thus, it presents a special challenge for those trapped in sex addiction.

Typically, addicts will try the 20 percent solution. That is, they will admit to a portion of what they have done in hopes that this will be enough to "do the trick." But recovery is an all-or-nothing proposition, and the acceptance must be total if it is to be effective. Addicts must be prepared to confront and accept every aspect of their past behavior and every defect of character if they are to recover.

This is often where the help of others—a trained therapist, an experienced mentor or sponsor in the recovery program, members of a support group—is crucial. They can help the recovering addicts ferret out and face the underlying issues that fuel their compulsions. They can help addicts overcome the guilt and shame in order to keep going down the path of freedom.

Search for God. After the addict has accepted his or her powerlessness, the next step is to acknowledge God as the central figure in the recovery process.

Not everyone reaches this point with the same level of understanding. Some will have had a lifelong involvement in a church. Others will have been convinced atheists with virtually no knowledge of God and His nature. It really doesn't matter. What matters as far as recovery is concerned is that the person honestly seek God and acknowledge that God, not himself or herself, is the source of power, healing and life.

The wording of the Second and Third Steps, with their references to "a Power greater than ourselves" and to "God as we understood God," is disturbing to some Christians. Indeed, even though the original Twelve Steps were written by fervent Christians, they were deliberately worded to allow maximum latitude for various views of God, in hopes of keeping religious arguments out of the recovery process.

As the years have gone by, this flexible wording has sometimes enabled recovery groups to adopt unbiblical concepts of who God is and what He is like. Still, the Twelve Steps can be, and usually are, applied in a way that is fully compatible with biblical Christian faith. At our own treatment centers, we emphasize that the "higher power" is God in Christ through the Holy Spirit, and none other. We emphasize that it was in the sacrifice of Christ that our past sins and hurts have been dealt with. Confidence in this saving reality enables us to share our problems, knowing that whatever we may have done is covered by the atoning blood of Christ.

Typically, our patients have previously adopted the common view of Christianity that it is nothing more than a list of rules and regulations that are impossible to keep. Helping them grasp the reality of the love of Christ is the most liberating thing we can do for them. When men and women realize that all their sins are forgiven and that Christ has already paid for them on the cross, no matter how heinous or numerous they may be, they immediately gain a sense of relief and hope.

All it takes is faith. Faith can free people from years of fear and anxiety. Faith can empower them to rise from the pit of depression and feel whole again. All that is needed is to make the power of God in Christ part of the acceptance phase of recovery. Jesus stands at the door of the heart of each and every person, knocking patiently, waiting for him or her to invite Him in (see Rev. 3:20).

The Bible promises that God will work in the hearts of those who invite Him in, to help them want to do what is right, and then to help them carry it out (see Phil. 2:13). Even those who were once alienated from God can come to see themselves as part of God's perfect, eternal plan. They find new meaning and purpose for their lives. Even though society may condemn them for their actions—even though they may condemn themselves—God stands ready to forgive and cleanse them. Indeed, the greater the sin, the greater the grace that flows from God's

> # The proof of acceptance is surrender—actually turning over every aspect of one's life to the care of God.

heart. Accepting God's forgiveness is crucial to the recovery process.

Surrender. The final part of acceptance is to actually turn everything over to God. The acknowledgment that problems are out of control may not be all that difficult. The acknowledgment that God can handle them—as an intellectual proposition—may also not be that difficult, especially for someone with a religious background.

But the proof of acceptance is surrender—actually turning over every aspect of one's life to the care of God. To recognize and be able to say to others that you are working under God's power and not your own, that you are seeking His plan for your life and not your own, is what fully opens the door to change and recovery.

Among the most comforting words in the Bible are those spoken by Jesus:

Come to me, all you who are weary and burdened, and I will give
you rest. Take my yoke upon you and learn from me, for I am
gentle and humble in heart, and you will find rest for your souls.
For my yoke is easy and my burden is light (Matt. 11:28-30).

What a relief finally to acknowledge that there is no need to take the
weight of the world upon our shoulders! Instead, we can take the yoke
of Christ, which is infinitely lighter. To desire this is good. To think
about it is better. But to actually do it is what God is after.

Surrender, the Third Step of acceptance, is actually the first step
back into the real world. So often we fear what God may require of us.
We fear He will ask of us more than we can deliver. We would rather stay
absorbed in our problems than face what God may direct us to do with
our lives.

But in recovery, we meet a God who loves us and who has a loving
plan for our lives:

"For I know the plans I have for you," declares the LORD, "plans
to prosper you and not to harm you, plans to give you hope and
a future. Then you will call upon me and come and pray to me,
and I will listen to you. You will seek me and find me when you
seek me with all your heart. I will be found by you," declares the
LORD, "and will bring you back from captivity" (Jer. 29:11-14).

Apart from this perspective, recovery becomes just another self-help
program, another coping technique. The goal is not merely to cope, but
to become spiritually changed—reborn into God's will and plan.

I believe in the power of God to change lives. That does not mean
that the people who come to a treatment center do not have a lot of work
to do. It does mean that because of the power of God, we have access to
a resource that goes far, far beyond what any of us otherwise possess.

If we do not help an addict tap into that resource, we are not really
helping that person to recover. We are merely sending the addict on
another futile effort to do in his or her own strength that which he or
she has so pathetically failed to accomplish so many times before. When

the power of God comes into the equation, the counseling, the science and the mutual support are all energized to make a lasting difference.

Confession

Confession is the second principle of recovery. As addicts enter the recovery process, they must tear down the walls of silence and secrecy that have isolated them from their family, their friends and even their own soul. Otherwise, they will remain trapped in the caverns of denial, where, in the darkness, they will inevitably stumble back into the addictive process.

Secretiveness makes wounds fester. Kept in the dark, the poison of addiction spreads through the whole of our being. A familiar slogan among recovering addicts is you're as sick as your secrets. But openness brings healing. Bringing our secrets into the light robs them of their destructive power. Recovery cannot take place until we take the risky step out of hiding and into the frightening reality of openness.

It is hard for romance, relationship or sex addicts to admit that their past relationships have been a waste—nothing more than a quick fix, a means of instant superficial gratification, a drug in human form. But I have watched the chains shatter and drop away as addicts have moved from accepting their relationships have been unhealthy to fully and freely confessing that they used and manipulated others for their own pleasure. It is never easy to face the dark side of one's nature, let alone to reveal it to another person. However, it is absolutely essential to the healing of the soul.

The Bible tells us to confess our sins to each other so that we may be healed (see Jas. 5:16). Taking this humbling step allows some very wonderful things to happen. First, it enables us to identify with others who have come by the same route as we have. At a treatment center, in the support group, there are always those present who can say, "I know just what you mean" or "I've been there, too." To find that you are not alone can be a life-changing discovery and a powerful motivator to continue down the road of recovery.

Confession also enables us to receive the encouragement of others. In recovery, no one is ever rejected for accepting the full ramifications of his or her problems or for sharing them with others. Just the opposite is true. People flock to the one who has opened up in this way and bathe that person in words of love and support.

Third, confession humbles us. It puts us on equal footing with everyone else who is struggling to recover. Very few people enter treatment without the idea: "I'm different"; "I'm not as bad off as these folks"; or "No one could possibly understand *my* problem." Confession is the equalizer. It binds us to one another with the cords of love and acceptance.

This is why we encourage people with similar problems to share with one another. When recovering addicts earn the right to be heard by sharing their pain, it helps newcomers to open up and share what they might otherwise be afraid to reveal. Where else in daily life can the man or woman struggling with sex addiction genuinely unburden his or her soul to another sympathetic person? Only in a Twelve Step support group or a treatment setting is the proper environment to be found. What a liberating experience for those who take the risk to open up, to hear from others that they have faced the very same temptations and conquered them through God's power!

In the Twelve Steps, the process of forgiveness begins with the "searching and fearless moral inventory" described in Step Four. Again, this is a biblical prescription: "Search me, O God, and know my heart; test me and know my anxious thoughts. See if there is any offensive way in me, and lead me in the way everlasting" (Ps. 139:23-24). This testing of our ways shows us where we have been wrong and where we need to ask for forgiveness from God, from others and from ourselves.

Step Five then directs that this moral inventory be shared with another person. This may be the hardest step of all, but it is absolutely crucial. Admitting "to God, to ourselves, and to another human being the exact nature of our wrongs" is central to the process of confession. It makes concrete and tangible the inner desire to be cleansed. "If we claim to be without sin," the Bible points out, "we deceive ourselves and the truth is not in us." But "if we confess our sins, he is faithful and just and will forgive us our sins and purify us from all unrighteousness" (1 John 1:8-9).

The bridge between confession and the next phase of the recovery process, forgiveness, is found in Step Six, which says we must become "entirely ready to have God remove all these defects of character." This is simply another part of the process by which we become humble enough to receive healing. God is the One who promises to lift us up through forgiveness.

When confession is complete, you have truly become part of the recovery process. You are, in effect, providing your own treatment by being willing to face the truth about yourself and deal with it openly. Confession is the ultimate abandonment of all attempts to fix yourself, to play God in your life. It says to God, to self and to others, "I am ready to start over."

Forgiveness brings the individual to a point of resolution regarding the past and clears the path to the future.

Acceptance brings a person to the point of humbly acknowledging the need for help and the ability of God to provide that help. Confession breaks the barriers of silence and secrecy, and opens the person up for loving confrontation and encouragement.

Forgiveness

Forgiveness, the third principle of recovery, brings the individual to a point of resolution regarding the past and clears the path to the future. People who have become addicted to romance, relationship and sex invariably suffer from guilt, shame and remorse. The path they have followed has left them full of resentment and bitterness. Often, they are also consumed with hate. They hate themselves, their families and even God.

In recovery, they *must* resolve this anger, resentment, bitterness and hatred. If they do not, these powerful emotions will draw them back into self-obsession and trigger the addictive cycle once again. They must learn to forgive—to release themselves and others, and even God—from the prison of resentment. They must be able to look every other human being in the eye without bitterness, anger or malice.

After going through this process, many recovering addicts say they have rediscovered aspects of their character and being they thought were lost forever.

Most treatment centers use several methods to facilitate the forgiveness process. Some people are able to simply recognize the need to forgive and "just do it." They experience an almost instantaneous change of heart toward a parent or business associate. For most, however, it is not so easy. They must undergo the often painful process of walking through the hurt in order to heal their emotions.

Many times, patients will write letters to those who have hurt them. These letters are then read to the support group, which is sometimes enough to break the grip of anger and resentment. When necessary and appropriate, the letter is actually sent to the individual, with the goal of effecting reconciliation. A long-distance phone call might also be in order at this stage. Whatever concrete actions are taken, there is also frequently a need for patients to spend time with a counselor, working through the negative memories and emotions in order to be freed from them.

One woman who sought treatment had been repeatedly molested by her grandfather. He would demand that they go on trips together, and her parents would make her go despite her protests. He would tell her that all grandfathers did this to their granddaughters, and that to talk about it with anyone would cause unnecessary difficulties. This woman lived with the shame of the abuse for more than a decade. Her obsession and anger grew with every passing day.

Finally, in treatment, she sat down and wrote her grandfather a letter, which expressed all the shame and horror she had felt, and all the pain he had caused her. She sobbed as she wrote, each painful word making her relive the nightmare. When she was finished writing, she went to the fireplace and burned the letter. At that moment, her anger, bitterness and resentment also went up in flames. She was able to forgive him. It was the turning point of her life.

Another method used to facilitate forgiveness is role-playing or psychodrama. This can be challenging, but it often uncovers and dissolves the core of the problem. In psychodrama, other patients play the parts of resented family members or old friends. The patient acts out incidents from the past that still hurt, bringing to the surface the pain that has been buried deep inside.

Psychodrama can be a wrenching emotional experience as deep wounds are drawn out. However, it is a favorite of our patients because the results are phenomenal. People gain new insights into their own motives. They are able to explore the thoughts and motives of the person who hurt them. They are also able to come to an awareness of how much grief God must have experienced through the incident—watching one of His precious children being harmed—and then grasp the immeasurable depths of His forgiveness, which becomes the source of their own capacity to forgive.

Releasing others from the anger, hatred and resentment we have held against them sets us free. It makes concrete the transaction described in Step Seven, in which we "humbly ask God to remove our shortcomings." While it may well be true that other people's actions have harmed us, what continues to hold us back is that we continue to hold on to these negative, destructive emotions. Letting go of them, with God's help, releases us.

Aside from resentment toward others, addicts also carry the burden of their own wrong actions and attitudes. The further they progress in recovery, addicts see more clearly what their addiction has driven them to do, and how wrong and hurtful these actions were. They experience the guilt of their sin with piercing clarity. One of the messages of recovery, however, is that we can walk in the confidence that God no longer holds our past against us. He Himself has said:

I will forgive their wickedness and will remember their sins no more (Jer. 31:34).

Through faith in God and in the atoning sacrifice of Christ, we have no need to fear retribution for what we have done. God does not want to punish us. He wants to free us from the deadly patterns we have become locked into. Coming to experience the depths of God's compassion and forgiveness is the bedrock of recovery.

Accountability

The fourth principle of recovery is accountability. Recovery requires action. It cannot remain merely a matter of gaining new insights or feeling better. It must become a matter of taking personal responsibility for what we have done.

Invariably, recovering people addicts look back on years of hurting, abusing and taking advantage of other people. Taking responsibility means unlearning these destructive patterns of behavior and beginning to relate to people differently. In addition, it often includes making amends for past wrongs.

The most common form of making amends is apologizing: admitting that what we did was wrong and asking the person we harmed to forgive us. But it may have more tangible aspects. We may have deprived someone of money or other items that were rightfully theirs, so to make amends to them means paying back what we cost them. Or we may have harmed someone's reputation; if so, we should do what we can to restore it.

Whatever the case may be, the important thing is taking concrete action in the opposite direction of the wrong. In asking forgiveness and making restitution, there is a deliberate turning away from what is destructive toward actions that will bind up old wounds and heal relationships ruptured by wrongdoing.

Steps Eight and Nine make this principle concrete. They call for making "a list of all persons we had harmed" and becoming "willing to make amends to them all," and then to actually make "direct amends to such people wherever possible, except when to do so would injure them or others."

This is nothing more or less than beginning to do unto others as we would have them do unto us. We open ourselves to a life of putting others first, rather than remaining obsessively focused on our needs, our wants, our problems.

Most people in recovery have little trouble making up a long list of people they have harmed. In some cases, it will be impossible to make direct amends, and in other cases, it may be unwise or unhelpful. Treatment counselors and addicts who are more experienced in the ways of recovery can be helpful in sorting this out.

Making restitution is the ultimate act of taking personal responsibility. It is a wonderful teacher, which underlines the importance of refusing to repeat harmful behaviors. Restitution helps make God's forgiveness tangible, and it helps prevent guilt feelings from interfering with the process of recovery.

Step Ten provides for ongoing accountability. It suggests that we continue "to take personal inventory" of our attitudes and behavior and "when we are wrong, promptly [admit] it." This is a practical way of remaining accountable to God, to ourselves and to others in the context of a support group. Belonging to a support group is especially important. Most treatment centers encourage every patient to become part of a recovery group where open confession and accountability to others is a regular feature.

Accountability prevents us from falling back into harmful patterns. It helps insure that any problems that do arise will be temporary setbacks, not major derailments. It helps guard against the complacency that inevitably sets the stage for relapse into the addictive patterns.

Love

The fifth and final principle of recovery is love. One of the hallmarks of addiction—not just romance, relationship and sex addiction, but all kinds—is absorption with self. Addicts become so obsessively focused on themselves that they lose touch with others—including God. It is only when they take steps to actively refocus themselves outwardly that they are able to regain the love they once had for God, for other people and even for themselves.

Step Eleven aims to realign the individual's heart. It speaks of seeking "through prayer and meditation to improve our conscious contact with [God] a Power greater than ourselves, praying only for knowledge of God's will for us and the power to carry that out." Note the focus on

God's will, as opposed to our will. That is the secret to recovery, and the secret to all successful living. To relinquish one's own plans and agendas, to submit one's future to the will of God, is the ultimate act of surrender and the ultimate key to recovery.

Prayer and submission are also the ultimate acts of Christlikeness. Everything Jesus did was in submission to the will of His Father. He was utterly other-directed, in two senses. First, everything He did was directed by another—by God His Father. Second, everything He did was directed to others, never to Himself. His death on the cross was the ultimate expression of both dynamics: He went to the cross because it was His Father's will, and He did it entirely for our sakes, not for His own.

The aim of recovery is to make the individual like Christ in both respects: (1) guided solely by God's will; and (2) oriented to the love and service of others. Step Twelve indicates how this focus on others is to be lived out: "Having had a spiritual awakening as a result of these steps, we tried to carry this message to sex and love addicts, and to practice these principles in all areas of our lives."

The very pain and shame and guilt addicts have experienced become the precious gifts they have to share with others. By being open about their own experience, both of addiction and of recovery, recovering addicts can help the next struggling soul find release and freedom as they have done. Thus, the process of recovery is brought full circle.

Practical Aspects of Recovery

These, then, are the principles of recovery as expressed through the Twelve Steps. But recovery is not just concepts and principles. It is by nature an intensely practical, tangible, down-to-earth business. Let's take a look at some of the more concrete aspects of recovery.

Time

Time is a harsh taskmaster. We cannot rush it, move it back, speed it up or make it over. It keeps its own pace no matter how badly we want to stop it, back it up or shift it into "hyper-speed," where we could accomplish all of life's dreams in a single day. No matter how hard we fight the clock, it will always win in the end. It can never be defeated, only accepted.

Recovering addicts have to learn to accept this reality. There are many days when they want to speed up time, hurry through the process and arrive at their ultimate goal of complete recovery right now. But it doesn't work that way. In the world of recovery, this principle has been captured in the familiar expression one day at a time. We cannot attain a lifetime's worth of recovery in a single day. We cannot even achieve tomorrow's sobriety today. The only thing we can get our hands on today is today.

H.A.L.T.

It is vital that the recovering addict take care of himself or herself in simple, mundane ways. Be aware of these circumstances that can trigger a relapse into addictive behavior:

· Hunger
· Anger
· Loneliness
· Tiredness

Addicts worry not only about tomorrow, but also about yesterday. In recovery, there is an urge to go back and fix all the hurts of the past immediately, but this only opens the door to guilt and shame. There may be enough time today to address some issue from the past. There may not.

We must be accepting of the reality of time either way. The only way to deal with the past is by focusing on the forgiveness of Christ today. The question, "What can I do today to become the person I want to be tomorrow?" does more to resolve the hurts of yesterday than a thousand hours of anxious human effort.

There will be plenty of time to make amends for the past and the rest of our lives to do better in the future. For now, the recovering addict must accept that time is always lived in the present tense, never in the past or the future.

Reality

After years of living in the warped world of addiction, reality can be a real shock. Sometimes the discovery that life can be bearable after all is a pleasant surprise. On the other hand, genuine love and authentic relationships can seem boring to the people addict who has bounced from one addiction-induced high to another.

In recovery, the focus must shift from the world as we imagine it to be to the world as it actually is—from the high of immediate gratification to the more strenuous but far more rewarding task of building authentic relationships; from the grasping dynamic of taking what we want to the loving dynamic of sacrificing ourselves for others.

Character comes from living within the boundaries of reality. Addicts are always looking for a quick escape, an easy way out. As a result, emotional development is short-circuited and character is undermined. Standing firm in the face of temptation, deciding to come to grips with reality rather than run for the cover of escapist fantasy, persevering in difficult times rather than seeking a destructive quick fix—these are the building blocks of mature character. The mature are willing to feel uncomfortable now in order to become better and stronger later. The temporary discomfort is soon supplanted by a sense of self-respect and the joy of knowing that reality can be accepted and lived in.

Change

Change is obviously welcome if life has previously been a constant downward spiral. Those in recovery long for change. But change can be a killer if it is not carefully understood and properly handled. It can be overwhelming: taking on too much too soon, trying to resolve too many things from the past and altering too many things in the present. Throwing ourselves into the whirlwind of change can make us dizzy, unable to determine which direction to go next.

Recovery often depends on developing consistency in the midst of change. Those who have never operated according to a schedule usually need to develop one, so that consistency can become a habit. Those with packed schedules usually need to lessen their load lest they lose perspective and go overboard. Change is a new reality they must learn to live with comfortably and productively.

One of the first things we tell people entering recovery is to defer major life changes for a year. Recovering addicts, in the first flush of freedom and the resolve to "be different," often think it would be easier to just wipe the slate clean and start out fresh, with nothing from the past to drag them down. So they divorce, separate, move, quit their jobs, break commitments and so on.

This is an extremely unhealthy way to make a new start. Recovery is about coming to grips with what we have done and who we have become, not turning our back on it. It is better to wait until our minds are free of obsessive thinking to decide which major changes will be healthy and which ones will only be escaping reality.

Sponsors

The most frustrating days I have spent working with recovering addicts have been days spent with those who are trying to recover on their own, by themselves. The overwhelming experience of all recovery programs is that it does not work that way. Recovery is a difficult journey, one that can be made successfully only with the guidance and support of others who have already passed this way.

In the secular world, people speak of finding a mentor, someone who can guide them in their professional life. In recovery, a mentor is called a sponsor. Sponsors are recovering addicts who guide others along the way.

Why People Don't Recover

The reasons why people do not seek help for their problems are as many and varied as the people themselves. But here are some of the common obstacles to pursuing and maintaining recovery:

1. Problem behavior attracts longed-for attention
2. The pain isn't great enough—yet
3. Fear of launching out into the unknown
4. Someone is enabling the addiction (message to the enabler: Stop it!)
5. Fear of exposure; guilt is private but shame is public; the only answer is openness and making amends for the past; this resolves the guilt and robs shame of its power
6. Pride
7. "Praying for a miracle" when God wants you to take action
8. Seeking a quick fix
9. Despair; leaving a relationship or "coming down" from a romantic or sexual episode; the return to grim reality fosters a sense of hopelessness
10. Physiological or biochemical dependency
11. Fear of failure
12. Fear of rejection
13. Fear of change
14. Running from reality
15. False sense of happiness; during an episode of addictive behavior, everything feels great
16. False sense of power
17. Fear of insanity if separated from the fix

Sponsors provide encouragement when the going gets tough. One phone call, one cup of coffee, one hour spent with an experienced sponsor can save years of wandering back into the wilderness of addiction. Recovery is often confusing and painful. A sponsor can help sort out the confusion and offer comfort and encouragement in the pain. A sponsor is an invaluable tool for recovery, one that can never be replaced by a book or a seminar. There is no substitute for face-to-face contact, which offers counsel, confrontation and guidance.

Spiritual Growth

Recovery is about growth. Frequently people enter recovery and feel better about themselves in just two months of growth than they did in 10 years of stagnant survival. This is all well and good, but if they are not careful, they become so consumed by their own growth that it captures them and becomes a god in itself. They become driven to know more, do more, be more—to grow faster than is humanly possible. This type of distorted growth occurs when the foundation for growth is faulty.

The foundation of solid, healthy growth must always be spiritual in nature. Genuine growth cannot be based on a foundation of health foods and exercise plans. Physical elements are important, but they are not enough. Social recovery is also important—healing old, destructive relationships or replacing them with new, healthy ones—but that, too, is not enough. Only growth that is rooted in spiritual reality will last. Only authentic spiritual growth leads to peace and serenity.

There are so many confusions in our culture about spiritual growth. To some people, growing spiritually means having faith in yourself. There is some truth in this, of course—recovery does have to do with rehabilitating self-respect. But on the other hand, misplaced faith in self is precisely what drives people into addiction in the first place. The solution to a problem cannot be greater doses of the problem itself.

Other people veer off into faith in others. They pick a hero or guru and try to grow according to that person's standards and values. Again, there is value in modeling ourselves after others who have progressed farther than we have in various dimensions of growth, but all human models are limited and will ultimately disappoint us if we try to follow them too far.

Still, others put their faith in faith itself. They believe that things will get better simply by asserting that things will get better. They place their trust in the notion that "every day, in every way, things are getting better and better." But to borrow an old saying, "sayin' so don't make it so." There is no inherent process built into the cosmos by which things just get better. Placing our faith in our own faith will lead to tragic disillusionment.

Those who truly seek spiritual growth will eventually make God the foundation of their lives. A wise man once said that there is a God-shaped hole in every human heart; nothing else can fill it. Romance cannot. Relationships cannot. Sex cannot. Human willpower only digs the pit deeper. We must invite God to take up residence in our hearts, filling our inner emptiness with His love and power, trusting Him to manage what has become utterly unmanageable.

In recovery, we need power to fight back the temptations that threaten us on every side. We have already learned that there is no power within ourselves that is up to the task. We need a higher power, a power outside ourselves. We need the power of the creator of the universe.

Where do we find Him? In nature, but not merely in nature. In the words of the wise, but not only there. Ultimately, we find God only in His revealed Word to us, the Bible. I believe we will not escape our obsessions or stop our compulsions until we place our faith in the God of the Bible.

We must guard ourselves against philosophies that run counter to the Word of God, philosophies that sound attractive but that in fact turn us away from spiritual reality. Many people today say, "We are all God." This is a dangerous concept for two reasons. One, it robs us of the knowledge of who God really is. And, two, it puts us back in the very spot that got us in trouble in the first place—trying to be God. Have we not already tried to run the world and found how pathetically inadequate we are to the task?

Yet there is a God who can run the world and who can be trusted to watch over our lives. This is the God who created all that is, who created us, who loves us and longs to be Lord of our lives. He has revealed Himself in the pages of the Bible. Recovery depends on our opening our minds, hearts and wills to His loving care.

Note

1. Pages 67-68, reprinted from the Basic Text of Sex and Love Addicts Anonymous, Copyright 1986 with permission of The Augustine Fellowship, Sex and Love Addicts Anonymous, Fellowship-Wide Services, Inc.

"The Twelve Steps of Sex and Love Addicts Anonymous" has been adapted from "The Twelve Steps of Alcoholics Anonymous":

1. We admitted we were powerless over alcohol—that our lives had become unmanageable. 2. Came to believe that a Power greater than ourselves could restore us to sanity. 3. Made a decision to turn our will and our lives over to the care of God, *as we understood Him*. 4. Made a searching and fearless moral inventory of ourselves. 5. Admitted to God, to ourselves, and to another human being the exact nature of our wrongs. 6. Were entirely ready to have God remove all these defects of character. 7. Humbly asked Him to remove our shortcomings. 8. Made a list of all persons we had harmed, and became willing to make amends to them all. 9. Made direct amends to such people wherever possible, except when to do so would injure them or others. 10. Continued to take personal inventory and when we were wrong promptly admitted it. 11. Sought through prayer and meditation to improve our conscious contact with God, *as we understood Him*, praying only for knowledge of His will for us and the power to carry that out. 12. Having had a spiritual awakening as the result of these steps, we tried to carry this message to alcoholics, and to practice these principles in all our affairs (emphasis in original).

The Twelve Steps are reprinted with permission of Alcoholics Anonymous World Services, Inc. (A.A.W.S.) Permission to reprint the Twelve Steps does not mean that A.A.W.S. has reviewed or approved the contents of this publication, or that A.A.W.S. necessarily agrees with the views expressed herein. A.A. is a program of recovery from alcoholism *only*—use of the Twelve Steps in connection with programs and activities which are patterned after A.A., but which address other problems, or in any other non-A.A. context, does not imply otherwise (emphasis in original).

CHAPTER 9

Healthy Love

Recovery is a simple process. We try to make it more complex than it needs to be. It cannot be hurried. Recovery and spiritual growth must unfold one day at a time. They advance in the quiet moments where we meet God and allow Him to touch our hearts.

There are times and seasons in recovery. There are periods of rapid growth and intense excitement. But there are also periods of dryness, when progress is harder to attain and measure. It is our perseverance during those times that cements the progress we have made, and strengthens and deepens our character.

Most treatment centers have found that they can work successfully even with the most hesitant and reluctant of patients. Addicts can learn to love God, others and themselves. First, they must accept that they have a problem, and then be able to share that awareness with the treatment team and with other patients.

Once they have opened up in this way, they are able to forgive and to experience forgiveness. They clear out resentment, anger, bitterness and guilt. They ask those they have hurt to forgive them. Then they establish accountability relationships with a sponsor and a support group. The love they experience motivates them to reach out to others in turn. Once this has happened, the individual is solidly on the road to recovery.

Staying Sober

The goal of recovery is to achieve and maintain sobriety. Here again the heritage of Alcoholics Anonymous shows through. For the alcoholic, staying sober is clear-cut and easy to define: no drinking. Similarly, with other addictions, the drug addict stays clean; the gambler stops betting; the smoker stops smoking. Sobriety can be defined simply in terms of ceasing these particular behaviors. Stopping, and staying stopped, are the goals. For these kinds of problems, the slogan "Just Say No" is appropriate.

Staying sober is more complicated with people addictions. The aim of recovery cannot be the complete avoidance of all forms of romance, relationships and sex. It is similar to the challenge faced by people addicted to overeating: They cannot simply give up food. Rather, they must learn the difference between healthy and unhealthy eating. They must eliminate the latter while promoting the former.

In the same way, for those addicted to love, the goal of recovery is not to become a hermit living in the mountains. The goal is to foster healthy relationships and eliminate unhealthy ones. One of the staff physicians on our treatment team sums it up in this way: "Sobriety means establishing and maintaining a balanced lifestyle."

Relationship Sobriety

Questions like the following can help determine whether a particular behavior will be likely to contribute to relationship sobriety or to people addiction:

1. Will I later have to deny that I did it?
2. Is it self-centered?
3. Is it abusive to myself or to others?

4. Is it inconsistent with my values?
5. Would I refuse to do it if Christ were standing here with me?
6. Is it an action without an underlying commitment?
7. Will I feel better or worse about myself for having done it?
8. Will someone else feel worse for my having done it?
9. Is this a waste of my time or the time of others?
10. Am I doing this to escape painful feelings of reality?

A yes to any of these questions should at least be a red flag that the behavior being considered may be unhealthy. When romance, relationships or sex proceeds on these kinds of dynamics, it is likely to be exploitive and addictive.

At the same time, staying sober is always more than the mere presence or absence of certain behaviors. It is not uncommon to hear alcoholics who have not touched a drop of alcohol in years complain, "I'm as clean as a whistle and as miserable as hell. Now what do I do?" Sobriety is more than just not doing certain things. It involves personal growth. It is not what we avoid but what we grow toward that makes sobriety meaningful.

As we have seen, growth must occur in several realms. We must look to our physical health. We must be concerned for our emotional, social and mental welfare. All of this must be undergirded by spiritual growth, without which none of the others can be sustained.

The key is balance. Romance, relationships or sex has been the dominant factor in the life of one addicted to love. Now it is time for this element to find its rightful place as part of a whole person, not as a tyrant that controls and consumes a person.

Healthy Hearts

For the addict, life is little more than a protracted struggle to survive day by day. Many recovering addicts find that their recovery program offers little more than another coping strategy—a better one, no doubt, than the destructive and dysfunctional strategies they were using before, but a mere coping strategy all the same.

Recovery is meant to be much more than survival, more than just another coping strategy. It is meant to lead to "a spiritual awakening," as Step Twelve puts it, to a rebirth of the heart. Healing a broken, empty heart and filling it with love—for God, for others, for self—is the goal.

> # Recovery is meant to be much more than survival, more than just another coping strategy.

The central truth of life is that God loves us. Christ sacrificed Himself for us out of love to make it possible for us, in turn, to be men and women who love. Entering into that love, making it our own, becoming able to share it with others—that is what recovery is all about.

Healthy Relationships

A healthy heart can enter into healthy relationships. Healthy relationships are central to recovery for romance, relationship and sex addicts. Recovery without healthy relationships only perpetuates the sinful self-obsession that led to addiction in the first place. In recovery, addicts must learn to shift their focus, thus becoming free to share intimacy with others.

A healthy heart involved in healthy relationships is the precise opposite of addiction. Addiction maintains a secret life marked by fear and control. Genuine love, on the other hand, is marked by openness, trust and the freedom to give oneself to another. Addictive behavior is a deceptive substitute whose effects last but a moment.

Healthy relationships, on the other hand, grow in depth, meaning and stability over time. The quick fix of addictive "love" must be replaced by the lasting value of a healthy, growing relationship of mutual sacrifice and mutual commitment.

Such relationships are not widely modeled for us in society. Most of what we see around us—both in the media and in our own experience—tells us that the goal of a relationship is to get all you can, and if you can't get all you want, to look elsewhere. It is as if a relationship were like a financial investment: You determine your goals, select the appropriate vehicle, invest the required amount and sit back to await the return. If that return is not what you anticipated, you simply withdraw your investment and take your business elsewhere.

Relationships don't work that way. They require commitment and patience. Most of all, they require the kind of love that can only come from a healthy heart, one that has learned to look to God as its source. It's not what you get from a relationship but what you give to it that makes the crucial difference.

There are many contrasts between healthy and unhealthy relationships. Taken together they chart a continuum between the secular model and the biblical model. Understanding these contrasts can help us understand how healthy relationships work and how we can grow toward them as part of the recovery process.

Reality Versus Fantasy

Healthy relationships are based in reality. Each person is aware of his or her own strengths and weaknesses. There is no need to hide or to try to fool the other. Each person is also aware of the other's strengths and weaknesses. There is no need to pretend that problems don't exist or to tiptoe around "unmentionable" areas. If the partner is weak in some area, he or she accepts it and helps accommodate or strengthen it.

Unhealthy relationships, by contrast, are based on fantasy. What could be or should be replaces what is real. The elements of unreality become the focus. The relationship is built on a foundation that isn't really there.

Completing Versus Finding Completion

In a healthy relationship, each person finds joy in sharing in the other person's growth, in playing a role in "completing" the other.

In an unhealthy relationship, the focus is on completing oneself. This selfish dynamic is at the heart of codependency. Too many people fling half a person into a relationship, expecting that it will be completed by the other. It never works. No one can ever meet such expectations. It is only a matter of time until substitutes are sought—either in the form of other relationships or in the form of dysfunctional and addictive behaviors.

Friendship Versus Victimization

A healthy relationship can be described as two good friends becoming better friends. The strongest and most successful relationships—even the most passionate and romantic marriages—have this kind of true friendship at the base.

Where this base of true friendship is absent, the relationship is shallow and susceptible to being marked by victimization. The one who is stronger uses the one who is weaker for his or her own selfish ends. Sometimes each partner, being strong in certain areas, uses his or her partner's weaknesses in this way. Mutual victimization is a poor substitute for mutual respect and love.

Progression of a Healthy Relationship

1. Attraction
2. Mutual interest
3. Enjoyment
4. Giving of self
5. Sacrifice
6. Love
7. Intimacy
8. Discernment of God's will
9. Commitment

10. Marriage
11. Sexual intimacy
12. Deepening trust
13. Ripening maturity

Sacrifice Versus Demand for Sacrifice

Few of the magazines that clutter the checkout counters of grocery stores publish articles extolling the joys of sacrifice. But no relationship can grow without it. Unfortunately, most of us are more accustomed to demanding sacrifice from our partners than to sacrificing ourselves.

I know of a couple that married, looking forward to the satisfactions of a sexual relationship. They had both waited until marriage before engaging in sex, seeing it as the supreme gift they had to offer each other. Once they were married, they discovered that intercourse was extremely painful for the wife. Both physical and psychological factors stood in the way of her ability to enjoy sex.

During the first three years of marriage, they had intercourse fewer than 10 times. Yet the husband never looked elsewhere for gratification. He sacrificed his needs and desires for the sake of his wife's. In time, she worked through her problems and was able to enjoy sex. She never forgot how patient and sacrificial her husband had been. The very thing that for many couples would have been a reason to separate was for this couple the bond that held them together.

It's one thing to love another when the going is easy, but character and depth are wrought in a relationship when love requires the surrender of preference and privilege. Nothing strengthens a relationship like sacrifice. Indeed, it often seems that the greater the sacrifice and the more thorough the death to self, the greater the potential for the relationship.

Our relationship with God requires sacrifice. His relationship with us required nothing less than the sacrifice of His Son, Jesus Christ. Building a relationship—or restoring one that has been ravaged by the effects of addiction—depends on the willingness of both parties to sacrifice for each other, without demanding anything in return.

Forgiveness Versus Resentment

Forgiveness is a miraculous gift between two people. A relationship nourishes when we are willing to forgive past hurts and disappointments.

Refusing to forgive is like carrying around a garbage bag full of past hurts. Every time someone makes a mistake, you toss it into the bag and carry it with you forever. The bag gets quite full as the years go by. In time, it grows so large and unwieldy that the relationship goes nowhere; the weight of the past bogs it down completely. You or your partner finally decide that the bag is too big to mess with anymore, so you go in search of someone else to connect with—presumably someone with a smaller bag of garbage.

There are no garbage bags in healthy relationships. Out of love, the partners take the hurt and disappointment of the past and burn it up in the flames of forgiveness. What greater gift can we give someone than to set that person free from the weight of his or her mistakes?

But all too often, instead of setting one another free, you remind the other person of all the times he or she has fallen short. You pull out the garbage bag and dump its contents on the table, thus focusing all your attention on the pains and problems of the past.

Carrying a grudge is like constantly demanding that someone pay a debt he or she has no way of repaying. Past mistakes can never be undone, and often their effects cannot be reversed. The only way to deal with them is through forgiveness. You must take the garbage bag and toss it into the ocean of God's mercy. The mercy that sets you free can thus flow through you to those around you. When you unlock others from a past they cannot correct, you free them to become all they can become, and you free your relationships to become all they can become as well.

Security Versus Fear

Security is a rare commodity in our world. Often people come from such an insecure childhood that they can only hope that their adult life includes a relationship that allows them to rest in the arms of someone who really cares. So much of life is lived on the edge of risk that we feel an overwhelming need for at least one relationship to make us feel safe.

Small wonder, then, that so many relationships are characterized by fear. We fear being abandoned. We fear being smothered. We fear not measuring up. Fear can be so paralyzing that—in an effort to meet our security needs—we lean even more heavily on the very person who victimizes us. People will cling tenaciously to a terrifyingly abusive relationship because they are even more terrified of not having a relationship at all.

The Bible says, "There is no fear in love. But perfect love drives out fear" (1 John 4:18). When we shift from trying to use others to satisfy our security needs to trying to meet the security needs of others, we find ourselves in a new dimension. We focus on their needs, not ours. We fill their doubts and fears with the reassurance of our consistent behavior. We calm their fears by being reliable. We become, in a word, loving—other-focused and totally selfless—the kind of love that drives out fear and provides genuine security.

Vulnerability Versus Defensiveness

In a secure environment, you are free to open up and be vulnerable. It is wonderful to be vulnerable, to do an emotional free fall and have someone catch you. That delightful taste of vulnerability enables you to open up even more, discover more about who you are and appreciate all the good that God has created in you.

In a relationship characterized by fear, just the opposite happens. There is a need to build up a wall of defensiveness. If you do not protect yourself, after all, you will be violated, robbed of your identity, controlled or smothered. The dynamics of defensiveness lead to death rather than to life and growth.

Honesty Versus Deception

There is no way to build a lasting, healthy relationship on a foundation of dishonesty. Honesty must be at the core of a relationship; there is no substitute. It is fashionable in our day to paper over unpleasant truth. We deceive those we love, rationalizing that keeping secrets is really for their good. We don't see ourselves as blatantly dishonest—just "discreet" and "protecting their best interests." However, the harsh fact is that we are either liars or truth-tellers. There is no in between.

Virtually all addictions are maintained under the cover of some sort of deception, which eventually is woven into a vast tapestry of lies and cover-ups. Inevitably, the whole tapestry is uncovered and brought to light. The question in the partner's mind then becomes, *Can I ever trust this person again?*

Trust, once destroyed, is very hard to reestablish. It doesn't bounce back overnight. Those who have practiced deception in the past cannot realistically expect their partners to regain confidence in them until they have proven themselves consistently honest and reliable over a period of time.

Dishonesty is a very hard habit to break. One of the main functions of a recovery support group is the accountability it provides, holding the recovering addict to rigorous truthfulness. Without accountability, trust and the restoration of intimacy in relationships are impossible.

Healthy Love, Sick Love

Healthy	Unhealthy
Reality-based	Fantasy-based
Completes another	Seeks to be completed
Finds a friend	Seeks a victim
Sacrifices	Demands sacrifice
Patient	Impatient
Kind	Rude
Forgiving	Resentful
Doesn't hold grudges	Seeks revenge
Born out of security	Born out of fear
Vulnerable	Defensive
Allowed to develop	Pressed to perform
Gentle	Combative
Honest	Deceitful
Satisfied	Restless

Hope for the Brokenhearted

Healthy relationships are hard to build and easy to destroy. Once damaged, they are hard to repair. Addiction seems to undermine authentic, intimate relationships more than any other force.

There is hope. Our motivations and desires can change. We can turn from destructive patterns to healthy, life-giving behaviors. We can recover from romance, relationship and sex addiction. We can have healthy hearts and healthy relationships once more.

Marisa, whose story is told in chapter 1, seemed doomed to self-destruct at the early age of 24. By then, her list of credits included dozens of twisted relationships, hundreds of sexual encounters, three abortions and the unmistakable symptoms of venereal disease. Utterly broken, Marisa entered a recovery program.

Eventually, she stopped her desperate search for a Prince Charming to rescue her from her inner misery. She began to enjoy life as her self-esteem grew. Later, she met Don at a church activity, an honest man with whom she developed a mutually satisfying relationship. Marisa and Don are married now and have two children.

Mark was not as fortunate. You may remember his downward spiral from habitual masturbation to pornography to a smorgasbord of sexual exploits. His addiction cost him his wife, his children, his job and his self-esteem. Mark called a sex addiction hotline the night his wife left him, but he never took the all-important step of admitting that he was powerless over his addiction and that his life had become unmanageable. As far as I know, his sad story continues to this day.

When Ben's wife, Donna, refused to bail him out of jail, he hit bottom at the speed of light. No more excuses. No place to turn. This was it for Ben. The time Ben spent in jail was the worst of times for him—but also the best, for there he began the long ascent to freedom. After his stint in jail, he didn't try to go home, respecting the fact that Donna didn't want him there. Some friends helped him find a place to stay and then brought him to our treatment center. Donna also sought help and support for herself.

Marisa, Mark and Ben—three people with a problem. Two of them faced it and are now leading relatively normal and happy lives. One of them didn't. What made the difference? Marisa and Ben finally came to the point of admitting their need for help. They began to face the terrible hurt they had suffered and the pain they had inflicted on others. They took the first step in recovery, and then the next and the next. They found powerful spiritual resources to help them overcome their problems. They shared their stories with others who had similar experiences, and in so doing, found acceptance and understanding. They learned to love and be loved, rather than to use and be used.

Mark never even took the first step. He couldn't face the pain of admitting what he had become. Mark's pain is still controlling him because he has never had the courage to face it.

If you are caught in any of the addictions described in these pages, you are not alone. If someone you love is trapped in the snare of addiction, there is no better time than today to face the facts. Honesty with yourself and others can begin the healing process. The grace and mercy of a loving God can complete it.

If you need to talk to a trained professional counselor, please call New Life Ministries at 1-800-NEW-LIFE.

Life-Transformation Guide

This study guide is more than an intellectual exercise to help you comprehend and remember the material in this book. For that reason, it is more aptly called a life-transformation guide. Any kind of addiction—romance, relationship or sexual—is an indication of something painful you are seeking to avoid or escape. These life patterns allow you to relate to others in ways that protect or distract you from being hurt. These emotional defense mechanisms are supported by layers of self-deception as well as the deceit of others. Therefore, you have two strong internal obstacles you must overcome to break free from your addictive cycle. You must find the motivation and courage to face the pain you have been avoiding. You must also begin to live in the light of truth, because truth is the key to freedom. Finding the truth is no easy matter when dealing with areas of self-deception where there is also a great deal of shame and pain associated with your behavior. I hope this book encourages you to dare to truthfully pursue a new and better way of life.

The questions and exercises suggested are opportunities for self-examination, revision and correction. The procedures are simple, but they are not easy. If you approach them with a willing heart and an open mind, you will take the first step toward true love that will satisfy the longings that addictive substitutes can never fulfill.

This guide is not intended to substitute for professional care. At the outset, I strongly urge you to seek help in working through these issues. Denial is a necessary part of keeping an addictive cycle or affected relationship going for any length of time. Therefore, those to whom these questions most directly apply are the ones who will have the most difficulty seeing their problems accurately. I urge you to immediately arrange a support network of trained, objective people who can help you break through the denial while giving you the necessary support and encouragement you will need to keep going. I suggest a Twelve Step group, a treatment center program or a professional counselor who is experienced at dealing with these specific types of addictions, or a combination of these.

Getting started: You will need a journal or notebook in which to write out the exercises, record your reflections and give answers to questions. Make sure this journal can be kept private (unless you choose to share portions of it with someone) to ensure a sense of security. Answer the questions as fully and truthfully as you can. In the margin of your notebook, next to the written exercises and answers, note the feelings that surface, emotions you struggle to keep under control or complete lack of emotion (where some might be expected) as you answer the question. If you find yourself unable to answer certain questions or to deal adequately with the issues and emotions that arise, you have not failed. You may have succeeded at breaking through the denial that will keep you trapped in your addictive cycle.

If you are concerned for someone else who seems to have a romance, relationship or sexual addiction, you can use the questions to try to evaluate and better understand his or her problem. However, also look to see a pattern of addiction in your own life that may tie into the addictive pattern of the one you love. If you are reading this book as a couple where one or both of you are dealing with issues covered in this book, you can go through the study guide together. Work through each section in self-evaluation and offer your observations about how you see your partner's behavior in light of the questions. No doubt conflicts will arise. These may bring the truth to light or help one or both partners recognize the need for an objective third party. This person can help you keep your relationship growing in a healthy direction while going through the difficult process of recovery. The notes kept by one or both parties can be valuable to a counselor should you decide to seek professional care.

You will notice that some sections are geared toward women, while others are geared more toward men. This reflects the typical occurrence of romance addiction as more prevalent in women, while sexual addiction is more prevalent in men. These are not absolutes. Please adapt the questions as necessary to help you evaluate your unique situation.

Where You Are and Where You Are Going

We start our examination at the end of the book, which can be a new beginning for you. From chapter 9, we draw the characteristics of healthy relationships contrasted with characteristics of unhealthy relationships.

1. Each item in the following list represents a continuum of attitudes and behaviors, moving from unhealthy to healthy. Rate yourself on each relationship characteristic on a scale of 1 to 5.

> 1 = unhealthy
> 2 = mostly unhealthy
> 3 = sometimes unhealthy, sometimes healthy
> 4 = mostly healthy
> 5 = healthy

> Unhealthy Relationships .... Healthy Relationships
> Addiction .... Health
> Secrecy .... Openness
> Fear .... Trust
> Control .... Freedom to give oneself to another

> Looking for a quick fix . . . . Growing relationship of mutual sacrifice and mutual commitment
>
> Fantasy-based thinking. . . . . Reality-based thinking
>
> Expecting another person to . . . . Sharing in completing complete you . . . . one another
>
> Victimization. . . . . True friendship
>
> Mutual victimization . . . . Mutual respect and love (using each other)
>
> Demanding the other person to . . . . Self-sacrifice sacrifice for you
>
> Resentment. . . . . Forgiveness
>
> Fear. . . . . Security
>
> Deception . . . . Honesty
>
> Defensiveness. . . . . Vulnerability (without being destroyed)

2. Describe in your own words how you distinguish between healthy and unhealthy relationships. Where do you draw the line between the two? What is your level of willingness to do whatever is necessary to move toward healthy relationships?

3. Fear may play a major role in deterring you from recovery. What do you fear may or will happen if you let down your defenses? List all your fears that make you hesitate at the thought of pursuing recovery wholeheartedly. Who or what can you rely on to help you face these fears and overcome them?

4. Every addict or person who lives a double life becomes proficient at deception. Are you willing to commit yourself to rigorous honesty?

5. In what ways do you still deceive others close to you, rationalizing that keeping secrets is really for their good?

6. Are you willing to first become honest with yourself and God, and then move toward becoming honest with those close to you? If so, complete the following personal commitment:

I, _____, commit myself to proceed in working through the questions and exercises of this study guide with no deception of any kind! I will tell myself the *truth, the whole truth, and nothing but the truth* (so help me God).

Signed, _____

If you are willing to affirm this commitment to someone close to you, someone to whom you will make yourself accountable, share this with that person and ask for his or her support.

7. Exercise: For each item on the "Recovery Readiness Checklist," list in your notebook the actions you are willing to take to demonstrate your willingness to change.

Recovery Readiness Checklist

a. I choose to stop playing a victim and blaming others for my behavior.
   Actions:

b. I determine to uncover the source of my problems and deal with the source.
   Actions:

c. I resolve to live life as a mature adult, taking responsibility for my choices and bearing the consequences of my choices.
   Actions:

d. I replace my unhealthy dependencies with surrender to and reliance upon God.
   Actions:

The Addictive Cycle in Your Life

People who seek to escape or avoid some inner pain typically do not rely exclusively on one addiction or form of escape. There are usually numerous ways one typically escapes, perhaps skipping from one form of addiction to another. Therefore, it is helpful to consider the addictive cycle in your life as it can be seen operating with any number of addictive/compulsive behaviors you may use.

1. Exercise: On the following list, circle any area in which you use or have used addictive behavior to alter your mood or help you escape: overeating, eating disorders, gambling, alcohol, drugs, spending, stealing, sex, excessive work, romance or people addictions, sexual fantasy or watching television. Add to the list anything else you are addicted to.

2. Exercise: Chart out the typical cycle for each form of addiction that you cited in your life. You may need to repeat this chart several times in your notebook. Note the characteristics of each phase (what it feels like and what you want at that phase). Identify what you do and how long it generally takes you to move from each phase to the next.

Phase of Cycle	Characteristics	What You Do	How Long Before Next
Obsession			
The Hunt			
Recruitment			
Gratification			
Return to normal			
Justification			
Blame			
Shame			
Despair			
Promises			

3. Use these questions to help you understand your cycle:
   a. What kinds of thoughts crowd everything else out of your mind until you feel like you have to do something to make the obsessive thoughts stop?
   b. How does your hunt for relief interfere with daily routines and responsibilities?

c. What risks do you take when recruiting your source of relief or intoxication?

d. What does it take now (as compared to when you first started) to find gratification?

e. What do you feel and tell yourself when you return to normal?

f. What prompts you to have to justify your actions to yourself? If you use other people, how do you depersonalize them in your mind to be able to justify your behavior?

g. Who or what do you blame for "driving you" to do what you do? What do you use to excuse yourself or explain why you are not fully responsible for your behavior?

h. How do you think others would treat you if they knew your most shameful secrets? When you are feeling shameful, do you gravitate toward others who also act shamelessly? How does shame create more loneliness and influence the start of your addictive cycle?

i. When you feel despair from relational addictions, what other addictions do you turn to in hopes of escaping the pain? Have you ever considered suicide as your only way out? How often are you depressed and where does it fit in your addictive cycle?

j. What promises have you made and repeatedly broken? Who is affected?

k. How long does it take before you begin obsessing again between cycles? Can you identify specific triggers that start the cycle again? (Watch for and note these triggers.)

4. Exercise: Consider how each pass through the addictive cycle impacts your life. How does each year you continue to be controlled by addictive/compulsive behavior patterns affect you? Describe how your hopelessness, shame and blame have increased. Describe how your conscience has ceased to function to protect you. Describe how your family or love relationships have grown more distant or insincere.

People Addictions and "Hooked on Romance"

1. Exercise: Keep a log for one week, noting when you escape into a fantasy world and what prompts you to do so. Identify what you use: romance novels, soap operas, pictures of someone you do not know (celebrity), pornography for romantic stimulation, your own inner world of fantasy superimposed over a real person and so on.

2. Exercise: Describe the following primary relationships in terms of where love (authentic, genuine, self-sacrificing love) is missing—your relationship with your mother, father, spouse, significant others. How do these deficits relate to your craving for unhealthy romantic or sexual attachments?

3. Were you ever used by someone to satisfy that person's quest for sexual gratification? If you were ever molested, have you brought all your secrets into the open and sought appropriate counseling to resolve the painful effects? If not, this is *necessary* to deal with any kind of addictive behavior. Call a counselor immediately.

4. How have you justified using another person in your quest to find security, relief from pain or play out the victimizer role you may have learned as a child victim?

5. How did you use fantasy at an early age to escape? What were you seeking to escape?

6. How did you use fantasy or masturbation to compensate for unmet needs of childhood? When did you begin masturbating? Is this something you do secretly?

7. How do you superimpose real relationships with a role you draw from your mental encyclopedia of romantic fantasy?

8. Does being the object of a desirable person's affection and longing offset an inner conviction of shame and low self-esteem? How have you violated your moral standards or cheapened yourself to attract the kind of attention you desire? Do you use drugs or alcohol to lower your inhibitions so you can pursue this kind of attention?

9. Exercise: Write out what you say to yourself when you justify your inappropriate sexual or relational behavior.

10. What do you do, fantasize or think about that you cannot share openly with your spouse (if married) or feel compelled to keep secret because your thoughts are shameful?

11. Exercise: List everyone who has confronted you about using him or her, being self-focused or not knowing the real person with whom you were in relationship? Note any recurrent themes about how you are seen by others with whom you are in relationship.

12. Exercise: List the sexual and romantic relationships you've had. Describe how you took time to build a friendship, get to know the other person and learn his or her thoughts, feelings, plans and dreams. Or describe the relationship in terms of the illusion you created, the "chemistry," mystical connection, instant intimacy, love-at-first-sight or ecstatic feelings of hope that they would fit the role you longed for someone to play in your life.

13. What primary commitments made to you were broken? How do these influence your belief that true commitment is or is not possible? What is your relational pattern with regard to commitments? How close do you come? What excuses do you use to avoid commitment? When you make a commitment do you also look for a way out or another relationship just in case this one doesn't work out?

14. Which relationships and disappointments associated with relationships hurt you the most? How do you plan to protect yourself from

being hurt again? How does your determination to keep yourself from being hurt make it difficult or impossible to have a deeply satisfying relationship of genuine love and intimacy?

15. How do you use (or look for) another's weak points or negative traits to tie them to you? How do you serve others in a way that creates a host of reasons they can't live without you? What kind of withdrawal symptoms do you experience when not needed?

16. Exercise: List the people who are dependent on you. What have you done to create or maintain a relationship of dependency? Have you ever sabotaged the recovery or self-sufficiency of someone you love? When they move toward independence do you panic?

Hooked on Relationships

1. What are you willing to endure (e.g., abusive behavior) or give up (e.g., identity, values) in exchange for holding even a destructive relationship together? Has your willingness to endure such treatment baffled others who love you? Are your romantic relationships like a master and slave rather than being mutually respectful and mutually beneficial?

2. What early rejection, neglect or abandonment in early life may cause you to fear being abandoned again? Have you vowed you'd make sure you are never abandoned again?

   How does fear (of not measuring up, rejection, rocking the boat, abandonment, being alone, being unnecessary) motivate the way you approach relationships?

3. Exercise: Describe your view of hope in your situation compared with the view others have of the prospects for your future based on current reality. Do you display inordinate patience and the ability to endure a bad situation without the faintest glimmer of hope for change in a destructive relationship? Are you overly optimistic, avoiding the painful aspects of reality by skipping over it to an illu-

sion that things will be great? Do people applaud you as a saint for putting up with a situation others would not tolerate?

4. Exercise: Things don't magically get better. Identify three relational problems you have and cite what you are willing to do differently so that things will change for the better.

5. Exercise: Draw a picture of the anger seething inside you and another picture of how you appear on the surface. How often do you say yes when you want to say no? What do you do with the anger this creates? Why do you pretend things are fine when they are not?

   How do you express your anger? How often do you suppress your anger? Why? Is anger an emotion that is off limits? During childhood, what were the consequences of expressing legitimate anger? Are you angry no one meets your needs although you don't directly express those needs? Do you have outbursts of anger followed by remorse and attempts to make things right again? How might this relate to fear of abandonment?

6. Exercise: What do you believe it means when someone is angry with you? Check any of the following:

   __ They hate me.   __ They will reject me.
   __ They will abandon me.   __ I must have done something
                                          wrong.
   __ I am a bad person.   __ I should be ashamed of
                                          myself.

   What are you willing to do to keep people from being angry with you?

7. Are you strongly attracted to needy or emotionally distant people? How do their needs make them a prospect to become bound to you? Is the main goal of your relationships to keep them going? Do you accept infidelity on the part of your spouse? Why? Do you fear losing the relationship by establishing healthy boundaries of fidelity?

8. Exercise: List the people you are in relationship with on a regular basis. Are you surrounded with people for whom you function in the role of rescuer, savior, teacher or protector? Do you gravitate toward relationships where you are desperately needed and lose interest in people who don't need you? How does this theme carry over into your work?

9. Exercise: Consider the long-term effect your relationship has had on those listed above. Describe how it has lead to continued dependence or toward independence and healthy interdependence. How do you react when anyone in your life becomes self-sufficient (e.g., kids growing to maturity, an addict entering recovery)? Do you grow angry or lose interest when they don't desperately need you anymore? Have you ever sabotaged, discouraged or undermined the self-sufficiency of those you care about? How do you help, encourage and support their self-sufficiency? Give specific examples for each person.

10. Do you "not have time" to think about yourself because you are so busy taking care of everyone else who needs you? What might be too painful in your own life to take the time to focus on and mend? Might this be one reason that you surround yourself with needy people?

11. How much energy goes into trying to produce the desired effects in people, elicit affection, make them feel guilty or otherwise manipulate them in order to tie them to you?

12. Have you lost hope of finding a truly loving, deeply satisfying relationship where you are loved for who you are? How did childhood relationships influence this conclusion?

Hooked on Sex

Sex addiction is progressive, builds tolerance and produces withdrawal symptoms.

1. Exercise: Chart a history of the progression of your use of pornography and other forms of sexual addiction. Chart a history of the diminishing level of satisfaction in what used to "work" for you and how much more it now takes to satisfy your cravings. Describe withdrawal symptoms that come when you try to live without sexual stimulation at your current level of dependency.

2. Exercise: Correlate your progressive digression into sexual addiction with the erosion of desire for intimacy and sexual satisfaction in marriage. Have you interpreted this correlation as evidence that you turn to outside sex because you're not getting what you need from your primary love relationship? Can you acknowledge that your escape into fantasy and sex outside of marriage causes diminishing satisfaction within your marriage?

3. Exercise: Identify how far you've gone in the three levels of sex addiction: (1) solitary practices (i.e., fantasy, pornography, masturbation); (2) sexually gratifying behavior involving another person; (3) criminal behavior (i.e., using prostitutes, stealing, being a voyeur, having sex with minors, practicing exhibitionism, using child pornography or child prostitution, and so on). How have you justified each new level of addiction?

4. Exercise: Describe your public self and private self. How do the actions of your private self violate the moral standards and commitments of your public self? Describe times when you've experienced a detachment from yourself while you crossed a moral boundary. What has "the other part of you" done that could endanger others (spouse, other sexual partners, children, other loved ones)? How do you take responsibility for protecting those with whom you are in sexual contact but who are unaware of the risks you present?

5. Can you identify the origins of your sexual addiction without blaming your behavior on someone else? Do you blame someone else to

relieve you of full responsibility for your behavior? Are you willing to accept full responsibility for your behavior? How?

6. Exercise: Which of the following actions have you or do you practice? Check those that apply.

___ done in isolation   ___ secretive
___ devoid of intimacy   ___ devoid of relationship
___ ends in despair   ___ used to escape pain or problems
___ victimizing (using another person to fulfill your selfish sexual desires)

7. List all the times you can recall when you were used for someone else's sexual gratification. If you were molested, how have you dealt with the issues related to being used in this way? Describe feelings of confusion because sexual pleasure and excitement were mixed with fear, pain, shame and self-loathing. What connection is there between the shame of being used in this way and your sexual addiction? Are you willing to deal with these issues thoroughly in a counseling situation?

8. Do you feel more comfortable with someone who is shameless in his or her behavior because you can "be yourself" at your worst with him or her and this person willingly participate with you? What have you done when feeling shameless that you wouldn't have done otherwise?

9. The Bible sees lusting in your heart as equal to adultery (see Matt. 5:28), acknowledging that the battle for the mind is crucial. Do you accept the Bible's moral standards? How does your inability to control your fantasy life, while knowing it is condemned by God, affect your view of God and your relationship with God? Are you willing to practice continual confession of what is going on in your mind to someone who will help you see your obsessions in an objective light?

10. How does insecurity along with fear of rejection and disappointment in intimate relationships trigger your choice of lust over love?
Do you feel you must suffer alone and never reveal yourself fully
because you fear losing the one you love most if they knew the
shameful part of you? Do you gain a sense of comfort from assuring
yourself that you can meet your own sexual needs without relying on
someone you love who might reject you?

11. Are you ready to acknowledge that you are powerless over your
sexual addiction and have no way to break free without God's
help?

12. Are you willing to face the truth to find real love that can satisfy your
true needs?

Origins of People Addictions

1. All addiction must be dealt with by addressing the source of pain
being avoided and medicated by the addiction. What were your
unmet needs of childhood including: affection, protection, attention and affirmation? How do early emotional deficits relate to your
use of sex or an insatiable hunger for something to fill your needs?
Are you hesitant or adamant (draw the continuum) to unearth and
explore sources from your childhood?

2. Exercise: Make a list of the key players in your childhood. Of all the
people who impacted your life (by their presence or absence) what
feelings do you have toward each one regarding what they did or did
not do for you and to you?

3. Exercise: List those who have hurt you through their presence or
absence, action or neglect. Of these, whom have you forgiven?
Whom have you blocked out of your mind? Whom do you refuse to
forgive? How have early relationships caused you to fear intimacy,
doubt your adequacy or have an uncertain sense of identity? How

does your addictive behavior make sense in terms of helping you
deal with your unmet needs and longings?

4. Exercise: Check any of these elements present in your relationship
with your parents.

__ sexual abuse   __ physical abuse
__ lack of nurturing   __ failure to notice your needs
__ parents lack of care about you   __ workaholism
__ parental absence   __ addictive problems
__ blatant codependency   __ intense criticism and ridicule
__ appeasement
__ "my way or no way at all" attitude
__ death or chronic illness of a parent
__ rigid expectations that were impossibly high
__ divorce, marital strife or domestic violence

Have you dealt with these issues in a way that resolves them for
you emotionally as well as intellectually?

5. How would you describe your family's communication skills? What
secrets were kept from you or were you expected to keep hidden and
unspoken in your family of origin? What were the painful realities
and shameful issues you were expected to keep hidden or even to
cover up? How did you learn the "don't talk, don't trust, don't feel"
rules in your family of origin?

6. How did you learn to numb painful feelings? Did you avoid being
penalized for expressing how you felt by shutting off your feelings?
What feelings had to be denied or suppressed? Do you often feel
emotionally numb? Are you unable to identify your emotions and
describe how you feel? Do you believe feelings just "happen,"
impacting you in ways you cannot influence or prevent? Do you
remain out of touch with your feelings until they become overpow-
ering? Do you feel tremendous pressure to find relief from intense

emotions? How does your addictive behavior help control your inner state of emotional turmoil?

7. Did you learn to lie in childhood by recreating painful realities with fictional stories you have come to prefer? Compare your version of childhood recollections with others who were there.

8. Do you hold God to blame for your childhood pain? Are you angry at God because no one protected you? What categories of people and life do you mistrust: God, life, men, women, clergy, Church and so on? Why? How have you sought refuge in religion or faith? Does your faith help you face deep issues that trigger your addictions or do you use your faith to escape the painful issues without dealing with them?

What Keeps the Addict Addicted?

1. List the contributing factors that allow an addict to continue acting out without confrontation and avoid the consequences of his or her actions.

2. Describe any behavior or communication from a spouse or concerned others that protects an addict from being confronted about inappropriate behavior.

3. Questions for a spouse or concerned others: Do you condone, ignore or minimize any symptoms of addictive behavior? How do you intervene to soften or deflect the consequences of his or her acting out? How do you tell yourself this relates to your love for the person? What options do you have other than to continue in the relationship? If these options are unpleasant to you, does the addict rely on your complicity because you are afraid of what the consequences might be for you if the person's behavior becomes known? What do you think would happen if you confronted the person with a demand that the addiction be dealt with? Are you willing to allow

the addictive cycle to continue unabated because of your fears? How could the consequences become more severe over the course of time? How many more people could be hurt?

4. Questions for the addict: How did lack of confrontation on the part of others contribute to the escalation of your addictive behavior? Do you blame someone for "not stopping you"? How long were you able to "get away with" your addiction before others admitted it was a real problem? What unpleasant reactions do you inflict on those who point out your addiction and its negative consequences? What have you been through that you believe entitles you to greater license than others?

5. Describe how your focus on your own pain interferes with your ability to genuinely love another person. Describe ways you take advantage of others and justify taking what you need because of your intense need to soothe your aching soul.

6. Exercise: Contrast how you involve yourself in developing real love on a day-to-day basis as compared with how often you resort to a quick fix by your addictive behavior. Compare the level of intensity in your relationships to the long-term development of intimacy. How are you equipped to cultivate genuine intimacy? Do you settle for intensity because you are not prepared for intimacy? What can you do to begin learning to develop intimate relationships? Are you willing?

7. Exercise: Check any symptoms of unresolved pain that you have:

__ recurrent depression   __ panic disorders
__ psychological disorders   __ emotional stress
__ irrational fears
__ stress-related physical illness
__ you continually push yourself at an intense pace in an attempt to distract yourself from emotions or to keep buried emotions from resurfacing

__ chronic pain or ill health that defies diagnosis of a physical origin

When and how will you explore the origins of these symptoms to get to the potential source of your addictive behavior?

8. Exercise: Identify any of these symptoms of the fear of abandonment that apply to you.

__ clinging to a parent, even an abusive parent, in childlike ways even though you are an adult

__ clinging to an abusive partner or one who continues to endanger you by addictive behavior

__ seeing abuse and addiction as a comforting sign of need for you because you believe someone who is flawed and needy will be less likely to abandon you if you meet his or her needs

__ seeking out more than one partner (even emotionally having a relationship you plan to go to if the current one fails) to make sure you are not left without someone

9. Exercise: Human beings have these basic needs—security, belonging and attachment. Correlate your legitimate needs with the addictive or illegitimate ways of trying to meet them without the risk of intimacy.

10. Go back and read the list of typical high-risk behaviors of sex addicts on page 139. Which of these have you done? How has the level of risk you take escalated or diminished? Who else do you put at risk when you act out? (Ask an objective person to elaborate on your list.) How has your recognition of the real dangers diminished as your addictive cycle progressed? What risky behaviors excite you and cause you to obsess over the thought of trying to get away with them? Would risk-enhancement explain otherwise inexplicable behaviors?

11. In what ways do you try to deny the full extent of your behavior:

___ when confronted, suggest that the observer didn't see properly or didn't understand fully

___ continually redefine what level of behaviors are "normal" so that what I do is barely within boundaries in my own mind

___ continually redefine reality and the rules

___ refuse to get medical examinations after every incidence of sex with someone with whom I don't have a monogamous relationship

___ neglect to practice safe sex when I am acting out (as though the risky behavior my private self engages in can't affect the other part of me)

12. When someone asks, "Can't you see what you are doing to yourself and your family?" do you say, "I don't know what you are talking about?"

13. The Bible says, "If we claim to be without sin, we deceive ourselves and the truth is not in us" (1 John 1:8). How does this Scripture apply to you?

Living with Addiction (or Deciding Not to Live with Addiction)

1. For the spouse: What evidence of a double life will you take note of in the future (review the chart on page 161)? Do you notice when he or she seems somehow different, more distant, aloof? When things seem to be going wrong, are you willing to speak to the addict about his or her symptoms? When your spouse seems overly attentive or generous, are you willing to ask whether he or she has "fallen off the wagon"? Are you willing to stand your ground even if the addict accuses you of not being appreciative? Do you fear (or have you experienced) being tagged as a "coconspirator" if your spouse is a confirmed sex addict? How does your insecurity play into your reticence to bring to light the

truth about what your spouse may be doing? Does your spouse hold this over you as a threat or means of manipulation? Does fear that your spouse's addictive behavior is somehow your fault keep you from requiring him or her to get professional help? Has your spouse used this fear to keep you from seeking help for yourself?

2. Exercise: Describe the contrast between love and lust as you understand it. Do you think it is possible for your spouse to love you and yet violate the promises and sanctity of marriage when lust is out of control? Are you willing to affirm your love if your spouse will confront his or her problems with lust?

3. Are you willing to educate yourself and, if need be, work with a therapist to get freed from the prison of false blame? Will you shift your focus from doubting yourself to see this as your spouse's problem? Are you willing to learn what you can do to support your spouse's dealing with issues without deflecting blame to yourself? Are you willing to explore your own issues that may have prompted you to enable your spouse to continue in the addictive cycle without confrontation? What will you do to educate yourself? Which books will you read from the bibliography?

4. Exercise: Make a commitment to take care of yourself, regardless of what your spouse does or does not do to deal with his or her addictions. Which of these will you take action to do immediately?

___ join a support group of people who understand sexual addiction
___ refuse to accede to your spouse's unhealthy sexual demands
___ never tolerate abusive behavior
___ never have unprotected sex without verifiable proof that your spouse is free of disease
___ get a medical examination to make sure you have not contracted a sexually transmitted disease
___ never cover up for inexplicable or addictive behavior, lie or make excuses

__ continually confront dishonesty and self-deception with reality

__ refuse to let your spouse define what is "normal" or put you at fault

__ require your spouse to accept full responsibility for his or her actions

__ insist on counseling, honesty, accountability and some form of recovery program tied into a group that will not be fooled or bullied by delusions or attempts to control the perception of reality

5. Exercise: Create a plan—describe precisely what action you would expect the addict to take to get help and enter recovery. Plan specifically what you will do if the addict refuses to take action to deal thoroughly with the addictive behavior. Prepare to implement your plan. Know where you will go, how much money you will need to take care of yourself and your children, how you will support yourself and what you will require of the addict to reconcile. Write out your plan and begin working toward it so that you have options.

6. For the addict: Evaluate what your addictive behavior has cost you and your family. Compare this to an evaluation done by your spouse or someone who knows you well. What have you been robbed of because of your addiction: a relationship with God, self-respect, family, time, reputation or a job? What else? What do you risk if you seek help? Are you willing to take this healthy risk in order to preserve your family, self-respect, health, and hope of love and genuine intimacy?

7. Exercise: Since addicts are proficient at making up new rules of what is acceptable, you need to have a set of moral absolutes to help you face your wrong behavior and know when you need to turn for help. Use the Ten Commandments to evaluate your behavior (see Exod. 20:1-17). Which of these moral absolutes God sets out have you crossed in protecting and promoting your addictive behavior? Write out a full confession of how you have broken any of the Ten Commandments as part of your addictive cycle. Are you willing to acknowledge that you are powerless to keep God's laws? Are you willing to ask Him for help?

8. Exercise: Are you willing to go to the doctor to be thoroughly checked for sexually transmitted diseases? Will you make a firm commitment to make sure you are not carrying a STD after each incidence of acting out that involves contact with another person?

9. Exercise: This book has helped you think about and examine the issues related to people, relationships, romance and sexual addictions. You cannot deal with these kinds of problems sufficiently on your own. Are you willing to take immediate action to confront all the issues you have touched on in this book and enter the road to recovery? If so, call for help now! Call a local recovery group or 1-800-NEW-LIFE for a referral.

I hope and pray that this book has helped you begin your journey toward true love and genuine intimacy. We have seen many people find the kind of freedom you seek. If you are willing to pursue a way of life free from these addictions, there are people waiting to help you. Reach out for help today. I commend you for your courage, and I offer my prayers and hopes for your success.

Relationship Addiction Inventory

An assessment questionnaire for relationship addiction.[1]

1. Do you sense that your thoughts and/or behaviors relative to your partner and your relationship with him or her are causing problems in your life?

2. Have thoughts about your relationship with your partner interfered with your ability to function at work or at school?

3. Do you fail to meet commitments or fail to carry out responsibilities because of your relationship?

4. Do you struggle to control or completely stop certain thoughts or behaviors related to your partner and your relationship with him or her?

5. Do you focus on your partner and your relationship with him or her in order to escape, deny or numb your feelings?

6. Do you think about your partner more or less than you would like to?

7. Have you taken financial risks with your own resources by giving or loaning your partner money for his or her sexual activities?

8. Does it seem as though there is another person or force inside of you that drives you to get into or stay in relationships?

9. Do you have two standards of fidelity—one for yourself and one for your partner/spouse?

10. Do you think you would be happy if only you could give your partner enough sex and/or just the right kind of sex?

11. Do you feel empty or shameful after having sexual fantasies or engaging in sexual activities with your partner?

12. Do you feel obligated to have sex?

13. Have you ever promised yourself that you would never again have another sexual relationship?

14. Do you find it necessary to fantasize or distract yourself in some way during sexual activity?

15. Do you dress in such a way as to make your body appear undesirable?

16. Do you set rules regarding when, how or with whom you can be sexual, and then break those rules?

17. Do you focus on your relationship in order to deal with, deny or avoid problems in your life?

18. Does your partner use threats or promises in order to have sexual activity with you?

19. Do you sometimes find yourself flirting with someone or being sexual with someone and wondering how it happened?

20. Have you stayed in a marriage or other relationship only because you thought that no one else would want you?

21. Do you think that your sexual abilities are the most important qualities you have to offer another person?

22. Do you dread or fear trips out of town because of what you think your partner might do sexually while you're away?

23. When you have child care responsibilities, do you put a higher priority on your partner than you do on the welfare of the child(ren) in your care?

24. Does your relationship interfere with your spiritual or religious life? Does your behavior in your relationship cause you to believe that you don't deserve to have a religious or spiritual life?

25. Have you sought medical attention for injuries related to your sexual activities?

26. Are you afraid to leave your partner alone with children, for fear that sexual contact might take place?

27. Has your relationship ever led you to consider suicide or self-mutilation?

28. When you are in a relationship with someone, do you try to make sure that another sex partner will be available to you, in case anything goes wrong with the first relationship?

29. Do you spend time with or have sex with people you don't even like or respect because you feel it is better than being alone?

30. Do you stay in unsatisfying, painful, humiliating, neglectful, disrespectful or otherwise unhealthy relationships only so that you can continue to be sexual with someone?

31. Are you unhappy or uncomfortable with your partner's need for sex or the nature of the sexual behavior he or she desires?

32. Are you afraid to say no to sex with your partner? Are you afraid to refuse to participate in certain sexual activities with him or her?

33. Do you consent to have sex with your partner even when you are ill or otherwise not feeling well?

34. Do you either minimize or exaggerate the facts when discussing your sexual life with others?

35. Does your partner initiate sexual activity with you before you are awake?

36. Do you have chronic medical problems with your sex organs?

37. Do you jeopardize your own safety and/or health by not taking reasonable precautions or by going to unsafe places in order to please your partner?

38. Have you lost a job or risked losing a job because of your preoccupation with a relationship?

39. Does your relationship cause you to violate your ethical standards, principles and/or the oaths of your profession?

40. Do you scan printed material (novels, newspapers, magazines) so that you can find and then hide or dispose of the things that you think might sexually stimulate your partner?
41. Have you been injured due to the frequency, intensity or nature of sexual activity you participate in with your partner?
42. Have your sexual behaviors led to hospitalization?

Note
   1. Taken from *What Everyone Needs to Know About Sex Addiction* (Minneapolis, MN: CompCare Publishers, 1989), pp. 39-42. Used by permission.

Sexual Addiction Assessment

An assessment questionnaire for sexual addiction—developed by sexual addicts.[1]

1. Do you sense that your sexual thoughts and/or behaviors are causing problems in your life?
2. Have sexual thoughts interfered with your ability to function at work or at school?
3. Do you worry that your sexual thoughts and/or behaviors are more powerful than you are?
4. Do you sometimes think that you are the only person who has certain sexual thoughts or engages in certain sexual behaviors?
5. Do you fail to meet commitments or fail to carry out responsibilities because of your sexual behaviors?
6. Do you struggle to control or to completely stop your sexual thoughts and/or behaviors?

7. Do you fantasize about sex, or masturbate, or engage in sexual activity with another person in order to escape, deny or numb your feelings?

8. Do you think about sex either more or less than you would like to?

9. Do you think of yourself as a person who has no sexual thoughts or desires whatsoever?

10. Do you think that there is something wrong or abnormal regarding the frequency of sexual activity that you have or wish to have?

11. Do you spend more money than you can afford to spend on sexual activities?

12. Does it seem as though there is another person or force inside you that drives you to be sexual?

13. Do you have two standards of fidelity—one for yourself and one for your partner?

14. Do you think you would be happy if only you had enough sex and/or just the right sex partner(s)?

15. Do you feel empty or shameful after having sexual fantasies or engaging in sexual activity?

16. Do you feel obligated to have sex?

17. Have you ever promised yourself that you would never again have another sexual relationship?

18. Do you find it necessary to fantasize during sexual activity?

19. Do you set rules regulating the frequency of your sexual thoughts and activities?

20. Do you dress in such a way as to make your body appear undesirable?

21. Do you set rules regarding when, how or with whom you can be sexual, and then break those rules?

22. Do you use sexual thoughts and/or behaviors to deal with, deny or avoid problems in your life?

23. Do you use threats or promises in order to have sexual activity with another person?

24. Do you sometimes find yourself being sexual or flirting with someone and wondering how it happened?

25. Do you risk legal problems in order to be sexual?

26. Have you stayed in a marriage or other relationship only because you thought that relationship somehow protected you from being promiscuous?

27. Do you think that your sexual abilities are the most important qualities you have to offer another person?

28. Are you fearful of seeking medical attention for injuries related to your sexual activities?

29. Do you anxiously anticipate or fear trips out of town because of what you think you might do sexually while you're away?

30. When you have child care responsibilities, do you put a higher priority on masturbating or being sexual than you do on the welfare of the child(ren) in your care?

31. Do your sexual thoughts and/or behaviors interfere with your spiritual or religious life? Do your sexual thoughts and/or behaviors cause you to believe that you don't deserve to have a religious or spiritual life?

32. Are you afraid to be left alone with children, for fear of being sexual with them?

33. Have your sexual thoughts and/or behaviors led you to consider suicide, castration or self-mutilation?

34. When you are in a relationship with someone, do you try to make sure that another sex partner will be available to you in case anything goes wrong with the first relationship?

35. Do you stay in unsatisfying, painful, humiliating or otherwise unhealthy relationships only so that you can continue to be sexual with someone?

36. Do you spend time with people you don't even like or respect, hoping that you will have an opportunity to be sexual with them?

37. Do you have sex with your partner even when he or she is ill?

38. Does your sexual partner complain about your need for sex or your sexual behaviors? Does he or she refuse to participate in certain sexual activities with you?

39. Do you either minimize or exaggerate the facts when discussing your sexual life with others?

40. Have you ever tried to stop your sexual activity in an effort to end a painful relationship or behavior pattern?

41. Do you initiate sexual activity with a partner before he or she is awake?

42. Do you have chronic medical problems with your sex organs?

43. Do you put yourself in danger by not taking reasonable precautions or by going to unsafe places in order to have sex?

44. Have you lost a job or risked losing a job because of your sexual behaviors?

45. Do your sexual behaviors cause you to violate the ethical standards, principles and/or oaths of your profession?

46. Do you scan printed material (novels, newspapers, magazines) or change channels on the television set just to find something that will stimulate you sexually?

47. Do you regularly engage in fantasies involving self-abuse or other kinds of physical abuse?

48. Do you trade material things (dinner, drugs, money) for sex?

49. Do your sexual behaviors lead you to risk injury, illness or death?

50. Have your sexual behaviors led to treatment or hospitalization?

51. Do you masturbate after having sex?

52. Have you injured yourself due to the frequency, intensity or nature of your masturbation or other sexual activities?

53. Would you rather masturbate than be sexual with a partner?

54. Do you spend time looking through windows, hoping that you might see something that will stimulate you sexually?

55. Do you follow people on the street, pick up hitchhikers or drive around in your car, hoping that these activities will lead to sexual encounters?

56. Do you undress, masturbate or engage in sexual activities in places where strangers are likely to see you?

57. Do you feel compelled to dress a certain way or to take part in certain rituals in order to masturbate or be sexual with another person?

58. Do you seek out crowds so that you can rub against people or otherwise be in close physical contact with strangers?

59. Do you make phone calls to strangers in order to talk about sex or masturbate?

60. Do you masturbate while driving?

61. Have you ever been sexual with animals?
62. Have you replaced a collection of pornographic material after destroying one collection and vowing never to purchase pornography again?
63. Do you masturbate or engage in sexual activity with partners in public places?
64. Do you steal money in order to engage in sexual activities?
65. Has an important relationship in your life ended because of your inability to stop being sexual outside of that relationship?

Note
1. Taken from *What Everyone Needs to Know About Sex Addiction* (Minneapolis, MN: CompCare Publishers, 1989). Used by permission.

Family History Questionnaire

This list of questions can help you determine the roots of your addiction.[1]

Addictions and Compulsive Behavior

1. Do you now recognize any kind of addictive pattern in your family? In your parents' families (i.e., among your grandparents)? Were there alcohol problems, gambling, workaholism or other kinds of addictive or compulsive behavior? When did you first learn of this problem? During your childhood? Or only recently?

2. Did your family live by the same rules that govern an alcoholic or addictive household: "Don't trust, don't talk, don't feel"? What special rules—unique to your family—did you learn as a child?

3. Was your family really normal, or did you just think it was normal? If your family tried to hide family problems behind a "normal" facade, how much did this image fool you as a kid?

4. Did you ever wish you had been born into another family? Did you seek out other families?

5. Did you ever have any sustained feelings that you wished something bad would happen to somebody in your family?

6. Was there a certain constant chaos in your family that other families didn't seem to have? Or was your family really overprotective and worried about everything, always worried to death about what everybody else was doing and how they were feeling?

7. Do you feel your family was "too close," "not close enough" or balanced in between? Has there been a problem really being close to anyone else in your family? Do you all back off whenever you get close to one another?

8. Did your parents have work-related problems? Were your parents able to keep a job, if they held jobs, or did they always end up getting fired, or did they change jobs a lot? Did you always seem to have financial problems when you were growing up?

9. Did your parents have any persistent legal problems? Any arrests? How many? For what? Any pattern of trouble with the law?

10. Did your parents have marital problems? Did your mom and dad have fights or arguments a lot? Were they close? Were your parents warm and affectionate with each other? Did you ever see them show any affection toward each other?

Covering Up

1. If you recognized or now recognize addictive patterns in your family, what attempts did your parents make to conceal these problems from you and your siblings?

2. How successful were your parents' attempts to hide the truth from you? How long were you kept in the dark about the problem? Did you know more about what went on in the home than your parents thought you did? Were you aware that there was a problem, even though you may not have known the exact nature of the problem?

3. Did both parents participate in this cover-up of the problem where you were concerned? Who put more energy into covering up and

keeping the problem a secret from the kids? The parent with the addiction or compulsive behavior? Or the other parent?

4. Did the secret problem make your family's home environment seem unsafe? Did you feel insecure as a child? Did you feel unsure of yourself and other members of your family? Do you still feel that way about yourself or other people?

5. Did the secretiveness and the deceit used as a cover-up spread beyond the area of the immediate problem to other areas of family life?

Alienation

1. Did you participate in keeping the family secrets hidden from others? Did your family have other secrets besides an addiction or compulsive behavior? What were they?

2. Did growing up without talking about the problem in your family make it hard to talk about other problems as a child? Do you still find it hard to talk about your problems?

3. Did knowing there was a problem, but not being able to talk about it, make you feel isolated from people outside the family? Feel unique or weird or different?

4. Did you ever feel uncomfortable about having friends over to your house? Did your attempts to preserve these family secrets keep others at a distance? Did you keep other people at arm's length because you were afraid they might find out something was wrong with you or your family?

5. Did you ever have someone outside the home with whom you could share your feelings about what was going on inside the home? Did you feel isolated or friendless as a child?

Control

1. Did you try to control the tension you perceived in your home—whether aware of the exact nature of the problem or not? What were some of the ways in which you tried to control the tension?

2. Did you ever try to be perfect or good in an attempt to ease the tension?

Did you adopt a special role in the family in an attempt to keep everything running smoothly?

3. Did you take on extra responsibility to make things easier on your parents—and on yourself? Did you act up in an attempt to get some attention for yourself? Did you try to make everyone else in the family happy? Or did you just try to stay out of everyone else's way?

4. Were you ever blamed for the tension in your home? Did you quietly accept this blame? Did you sometimes feel you were a bad child?

5. Was independent thinking promoted in your family? Freedom of thought? Were you encouraged as a child to be your own person and to grow? Or were you admonished to toe the line? Did you feel totally unable to say no to anyone who asked you to do something as a child? Do you now?

6. Did you have permission to show your feelings as a child? Or did you learn to hide emotions as a child? All emotions, or just particular feelings? Which ones?

7. What happened in your family when someone did express their feelings? Did you gradually learn it was safer to shut down your emotions or cut yourself off from your feelings entirely?

8. Did you sometimes start wondering what exactly you *were* feeling? Did you sometimes not know what you felt?

9. What impact did this discouragement of feelings have on you? Does it still have an effect today?

Fears

1. Did you have particularly strong fears while growing up? What were they? Do they still affect your life today?

2. Were you afraid of trusting others? Were you afraid of what might happen if someone outside the family discovered the problem in your family? If you were aware of the problem yourself, were you afraid of outsiders ridiculing you if they knew, too? If you weren't aware of the exact problem, were you still afraid that others might discover that your family image was just a fraud?

3. Were you ever afraid that your parents might simply abandon you? Did you ever feel afraid that if you told your parents what you *really*

thought or felt, they might reject you? Were you afraid of your parents' disapproval?

4. Did you grow up afraid of angry outbursts or confrontations of any kind? Were you afraid of expressing—or hearing expressed—other feelings besides anger?

5. As a child, were you ever afraid that you were going insane?

6. Did sex frighten you as a child? If so, do you remember any incident that could help explain why it did? Does it still frighten you now?

7. Did you feel a general anxiety all the time—a fear of something that would or might happen, without knowing exactly what that something was?

8. Did you live in constant fear as a child? Do you now?

Trust

1. Did your parents—through both words and actions—teach you to trust or not to trust others? Did your parents behave inconsistently? Did your parents ever break promises to you?

2. Did the experiences inside your own home make it hard for you to trust others outside your home?

3. Did you distrust almost everyone as a child? Do you now?

4. Did you receive mixed messages from either parent? Or did one parent often contradict the other parent?

5. Did your parents ever contradict you when you made a comment about the tensions in your home, saying something like, "You must be imagining things" or "Nothing like that happened"? Did contradictions like these make you doubt what you'd seen and heard?

6. Did growing up in your childhood home make it hard for you to trust yourself? Did you feel inadequate to control the tensions and problems in your home? Did you feel inadequate in other ways?

7. Did you feel utterly powerless as a child? Do you now?

8. Did you or your parents set unrealistically high standards for your behavior? When you failed to meet these standards, did you feel you couldn't be trusted?

Self-Talk

1. What kind of things did you think about yourself as a child? Was your overall view of yourself as a child negative or positive? Did you feel worthless as a child? Do you feel worthless today?

2. How would you fill in the following sentences (more than one response to each should come to mind)?

   As a child, I was _____

   _____

   _____

   As a child, I was great at _____

   _____

   _____

   As a child, I was terrible at _____

   _____

   _____

3. What kinds of things did you think about most other people when you were a child? Was your overall view of other people as a child positive or negative?

4. How would you fill in the following sentences?

   As a child, I thought other people were _____

   _____

   _____

   As a child, I thought other people were better than me at _____

   _____

   _____

   As a child, I thought other people were worse than me at _____

   _____

   _____

5. What kinds of things did you think about the world in general when you were a child? Was your overall view of the world as a child positive or negative?

6. How would you fill in the following sentences?

   As a child, I thought the world was _____

   _____

_____

_____

As a child, I thought the world was good for _____

_____

_____

As a child, I thought the world was bad for _____

_____

_____

7. Have your essential views of yourself, others and the world in general changed since then? How would you fill in those sentences today—as an adult?

Sex Education

1. Recognizing that everyone gets some sort of sex education, what kind of sex education did you have during your childhood? What were the positive things you learned about human sexuality? What negative statements were made? By whom? To you directly, or did you overhear them made to someone else?

2. Where, when and from whom did you primarily get your sex education? In the home, school, from peers? What myths about sexuality or intimacy did you learn as a child?

3. What were the sexual messages you received from your parents? Not only the things that they overtly told you, but also the messages you received covertly, through observation of your parents and their relationship?

4. How did you view your parents' sexuality? What was their sexual relationship in the home like? Was affection shown openly in your family? Or not shown at all? Were your parents warm and affectionate with you and your siblings? Was touching one another something that never happened in the family? Were there negative statements about touching?

5. Did the environment help you feel good about yourself as a sexual person? Or was it a restrictive environment, especially where sexuality was concerned?

6. Did you ever talk to anyone in your family about sex? If you had wanted to talk about sex and sexuality, to whom would you have turned? Was there anyone in your family who might have answered your questions about sex?

7. If you were brought up in a religious environment, did it enhance your understanding of healthy sexuality? Or did the religious environment create greater anxiety about sexuality? Was masturbation expressly forbidden by your family or your religion?

8. Did any sexually traumatic things happen to you during your childhood? Incest or sexual abuse? Any traumatic or extremely humiliating incident? Were you ever caught and either punished or chewed out for masturbating? As a child, did you ever inadvertently see someone having sex?

9. Was anyone else in your family the victim of any molestation? Was anybody in the family raped? Have you heard of any incident in your family history? Any inklings at all? Did you hear anything about that? Or do you suspect it now that you look back and admit that maybe something was going on?

10. If there was incest in your immediate family and only one of your parents was involved in the incest, did you ever blame the other parent for not preventing it from happening? Did you blame yourself for the incest in your family? Do you now? Did you feel guilty about the incest in your family? Do you now?

Note

1. Reprinted with the permission of Pocket Books, an imprint of Simon & Schuster Adult Publishing Group from *Lonely All the Time* by Ralph Earle and Gregory Crow with Kevin Osborn. Copyright © 1989 by The Philip Lief Group, Inc.

Additional Resources by Stephen Arterburn

available at www.newlife.com

Every Heart Restored. Coauthors Fred and Brenda Stoeker and Mike Yorkey. WaterBrook Press, 2004. A wife's guide to healing in the wake of every man's battle.
*Companion workbook available.

Every Man's Battle. Coauthors Fred Stoeker and Mike Yorkey. WaterBrook Press, 2000. Every man's guide to winning the war on sexual temptation one victory at a time.
*Companion workbook and audiobook available.

Every Man's Battle Guide. Coauthors Fred Stoeker and Mike Yorkey. WaterBrook Press, 2003. Spiritual weapons for the war against sexual temptation.

Every Woman's Battle. Coauthor Shannon Ethridge. WaterBrook Press, 2003. Discovering God's plan for sexual and emotional fulfillment.
*Companion workbook available.

Feeding Your Appetites. Coauthor Dr. Debra Cherry. Integrity Publishers, 2004. Money, sex, food, work, ego—take control of what's controlling you.

Excellent Resources for Teens and Twenties

Every Young Man's Battle. Coauthors Fred Stoeker and Mike Yorkey. WaterBrook Press, 2002. Strategies for victory in the real world of sexual temptation.
*Companion workbook and audiobook available.

Every Young Man's Battle Guide. Coauthors Fred Stoeker and Mike Yorkey. WaterBrook Press, 2003. Spiritual weapons for the war against sexual temptation.

Every Young Man's Battle Video. Guardian Studios, 2003. Captivating, informative docudrama based on the book.

Every Young Woman's Battle. Coauthor Shannon Ethridge. WaterBrook Press, 2004. Guarding your mind, heart and body in a sex-saturated world.
*Companion workbook available.

New Life Ministries Workshops

Every Man's Battle. Biblically based program for men who are looking for God's wisdom in keeping themselves pure. In our five-day workshop, the men who attend receive education about the nature of sexual temptation and a practical, no-nonsense approach toward managing its destructive effects. Our goal is to equip each man who attends with the tools necessary to maintain sexual integrity and enjoy healthy, productive relationships. Go to www.everymansbattle.com or call 1-800-NEW-LIFE for more information.

Every Heart Restored. When a man is struggling in a battle with sexual addiction, the impact on his wife can be devastating. This one-day intensive workshop includes tools for coping with the betrayal, grieving the losses, rebuilding trust in the marriage, and education in the nature of sexual addiction. Go to www.everymansbattle.com or call 1-800-NEW-LIFE for more information.

Take Hold of the Victory!

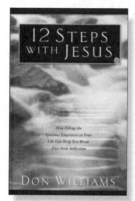
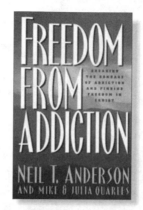

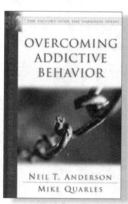

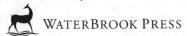

118 Daddy?

112 disinterested toys

112 co-dependent

113 Sharing yourself

111 Genuine Intimacy necessary to fully recover

108 Fear of being hurt

7/4/9
150 -